CROSSING
CULTURES

CROSSING CULTURES

Preparing Strangers for Ministry in Strange Places

STEPHEN M. DAVIS

Foreword by
John P. Davis

WIPF & STOCK · Eugene, Oregon

CROSSING CULTURES
Preparing Strangers for Ministry in Strange Places

Copyright © 2019 Stephen M. Davis. All rights reserved. Except for brief
quotations in critical publications or reviews, no part of this book may
be reproduced in any manner without prior written permission from the
publisher. Write: Permissions, Wipf and Stock Publishers, 199 W. 8th Ave.,
Suite 3, Eugene, OR 97401.

Wipf & Stock
An Imprint of Wipf and Stock Publishers
199 W. 8th Ave., Suite 3
Eugene, OR 97401

www.wipfandstock.com

PAPERBACK ISBN: 978-1-5326-8293-3
HARDCOVER ISBN: 978-1-5326-8294-0
EBOOK ISBN: 978-1-5326-8295-7

Manufactured in the U.S.A.   JUNE 12, 2019

Scripture quotations are from the ESV® Bible (The Holy Bible, English
Standard Version®), copyright © 2001 by Crossway, a publishing ministry
of Good News Publishers. Used by permission. All rights reserved.

CONTENTS

FOREWORD

IN 1973 I HAD the joy of seeing my brother Steve come to Christ. The gospel immediately began a lifelong work of compelling him to love and to serve his Lord and Savior. Together we have had the joy of growing in the gospel and partnering in church planting for over forty years. As a seminary student Steve and his wife, Kathy, assisted and served in our church plant in Bucks County, Pennsylvania. In the early 1980s our new church gladly partnered with his church plant in the Roxborough section of Philadelphia. Later we had the privilege of supporting him when he was called to church planting in France and Romania. Since 2009 we have had the opportunity to work together in planting a multiethnic church in Philadelphia.

When it comes to writing on missiological issues, we often find various extremes. We have those who have theological and missiological training but have no "on the ground" experience. We also have those who have practical experience in missions but have no strong theological or missiological underpinnings to guide them through the complexities of missions. Steve is neither of these. With two masters degrees in biblical and theological studies, and two doctorates, a DMin in missiology and a PhD in intercultural studies, he has the missiological and theological tools to evaluate the changing and challenging complexities in missions. Furthermore, as one who has been involved in urban church planting in Philadelphia, church planting and training in the postmodern, post-Christian climate of France, church planting and training in Romania, and theological training of pastors in many countries of the world, Steve is consummately prepared to write as one who has been on the ground and still has his feet on the ground planting and pastoring a multiethnic urban church in Philadelphia.

I would listen to what he has to say, not simply because he is my brother, but because I respect his training, his experience, his wisdom, and his commitment to seeing gospel-centered churches planted throughout the world.

JOHN P. DAVIS, DMIN
Lead Pastor, Grace Church Philly

PREFACE

GOD HAS GIVEN ME the immense privilege to serve him for over thirty-five years alongside my wife, Kathy. I continue to stand in awe at his grace toward me. I was raised in a Christian home, rebelled at an early age, dropped out of high school, entered a world of drugs and crime, and was no stranger to the police in my neighborhood in North Philadelphia. I was probably one of the least likely candidates to ever become a missionary. The joke was that my dad was a prison guard and we spent time on different sides of the bars. Yet God works in mysterious ways.

After my conversion in 1973, I went to Bob Jones University for four years with a GED high school diploma and on academic probation, and by God's grace graduated with honors. It was there I met my wife, to whom I've now been married over forty years. From Bob Jones I went to seminary for four years. My wife and I planted our first church in Philadelphia after graduation in 1982. The church called a new pastor in 1987 when we announced our decision to go to France. We left for France in 1988 with our two small children in tow to plant churches. Of course I knew nothing about church planting in France, knew little of French history, and could not yet speak French. Thankfully I had enough sense to work with a French church planter and eventually was able to function with some measure of effectiveness.

In 1994 my family left France for Romania—another ministry, another culture, another language. My wife cried when I announced to our church in France that we would be going to Romania. When I asked her later why, she told me it was because it meant learning another language. We went there with six-month visas. Six months later our youngest son overheard my wife and me talking about renewing our visas. His response, "You mean we're not going back to France?" In time Romania became home for our children, our French Yorkie, and the two German shepherds we bought after a couple of burglaries while we were at church. We sent the dogs and our sons to obedience school. I'm not sure how much they learned, the dogs or our sons. After five years in Romania, we returned to the United States, where I studied under Paul Hiebert, Tite Tiénou, and others at Trinity Evangelical Divinity School and received a DMin in missiology in 2004, with David Hesselgrave as my advisor. As I studied under missiologists, I had one regret. I regretted that I had not had this training earlier in my church-planting ministry and realized that I had not been as prepared as I thought for cross-cultural ministry. I am not an expert but I have learned from the experts. I have also had broad experience to share which might help others avoid some of the pitfalls I faced and mistakes I made. I suppose I could've entitled this book, *What I Wish I Had Known Before Engaging in Cross-Cultural Ministry*. I've written this with the hope that others might be better prepared than I was for cross-cultural ministry. Thankfully God uses us in our weakness and even in our ignorance. The pre-field and on-field aspects of preparation will not be the same for everyone due to differing gifts, calling, and places of ministry. Yet, I am persuaded that the call of God upon our lives requires the best preparation possible.

The changing face of world missions presents unique challenges, among which is the preparation of missionaries for effective cross-cultural witness and church planting. In an earlier ministry as missions director of a large church I was responsible for recommending missionary candidates to our church. It became obvious that mission boards and local churches often have different criteria for missionary candidates. In this book I draw widely from leading missiologists and practitioners. I also share many of my personal ministry experiences, successes, and failures. I want to try to formulate clearer thinking in preparing cross-cultural workers so that churches and mission agencies can better understand their role in world missions and their involvement in the lives of those sent. In doing so we must answer the following question: How can we communicate the unchanging gospel of Jesus Christ to unbelievers in the midst of a changing world? This is one of the great missiological questions of our day. Gone are the days when the isolated West sent missionaries to unknown lands and people. Apart from isolated ethnic peoples in yet unreached regions, the world has taken on more of a global character. Contact between ethnic groups, whether resulting from immigration, warfare and displacement or tourism, is unprecedented. Times have changed. We have more opportunities, more resources and are the benefactors of more past experience and research than any previous generation.

When I think of competencies for cross-cultural ministry, I have in mind specifically those who are called to plant churches, whether as a lead church planter, part of a team planting churches, or working alongside nationals to provide training and plant churches with them. No two places of cross-cultural ministry will be the same. The application, however, is for anyone considering or already engaged in cross-cultural missions since mission without church can scarcely be called mission. Anything called missions that does not involve gospel proclamation and discipleship with the goal of planting churches should be called something else. What that looks like in different cultures and how that is accomplished may vary. My prayer is that this book will help churches, prospective candidates, and mission agencies to more effectively partner in ministry preparation and gospel proclamation in making Christ known to the nations.

Introduction

NO GREATER DAY HAS ever existed than the present one for the church of Jesus Christ to carry out the mandate of her Lord as clearly given in Matthew 28:18–20, "to make disciples of all nations" (ESV). The twenty-first century offers unparalleled opportunities and abundant resources to effectively engage in this supreme task. Of all the earthly resources, none is more important than those who are called to the specific task of taking the gospel cross-culturally to those who have never clearly heard the good news of salvation and new life in Jesus Christ. Andrew Walls states that "one of the few things that are predictable about third-millennium Christianity is that it will be more culturally diverse than Christianity has ever been before."[1] If Walls's assessment is correct, then greater attention must be given to preparing cross-cultural workers for the complex challenges they will face in crossing cultural boundaries with the gospel. The divine dimension of missionary preparation can never be objectively studied and measured. The human dimensions can and must be examined in order to ensure that churches do not enter into the Great Commission task haphazardly. The gospel itself is not bound to one culture but transcends all cultures. However, those taking the gospel to other cultures, who themselves have had little exposure to or experience in other cultures, may be culture-bound and fail to understand how the never-changing gospel message must be presented, how new converts will be discipled, and how a new community of believers will take shape in another culture.

The challenges and complexity of cross-cultural ministry in the twenty-first century compel us to evaluate the pre-field

1. Walls, *Cross-Cultural Process*, 68.

preparation of missionaries in order to better prepare future missionaries. In our day, an age of unprecedented opportunity, we should not be satisfied with anything less than biblically directed excellence. Those who are entrusted with the gospel treasure, although "jars of clay," must allow the Potter to fashion them into vessels "set apart and holy, useful to the master of the house, ready for every good work" (2 Tim 2:21 ESV). This, of course, is a life-long process of which pre-field preparation is only a part. Andrew Kirk states that "when considering Christian mission everyone is obliged to work with traditions that they have chosen to believe are more or less compelling."[2] However, traditional practices need to be open to scrutiny and development. Samuel Escobar observes that "there has sometimes been a misplaced zeal to preserve cultural forms of previous generations with no regard for cultural changes."[3] This applies to models and methods of missionary preparation.

One of the most important things we must remember is that although we might leave our cultural comfort zone as experts we arrive in a cultural war zone as strangers, to not say idiots. Cross-cultural ministry is a journey into the unknown. Crossing into another culture is not merely entering another country by sea or air. People do that all the time. We call them tourists and business people. They land in another culture, have some interaction with the locals in their own language or with a translator, and delight in or avoid the strange practices and foods. They have entered the culture. They have not crossed into it. Crossing into a culture requires learning about the culture—the people, their history, their language, their food, their way of life, their religious commitments—and engaging the culture on more than a tourist level. Some tourists do all they can to avoid the locals and are content to eat, play, and stay cut off from the people who actually live there. Crossing into another culture for ministry involves engagement with people, people you do not understand, people who seem to have strange practices—why do French people kiss each other on

2. Kirk, "Christian Mission," 158.

3. Escobar, *New Global Mission*, 81.

the cheek several times, why do people not smile in public like friendly Americans, why do people speak with their hands, are they angry? And oh no, that lady has a dog at her table in a fine restaurant. Isn't that disgusting?

In some ways you will always be a stranger in a strange place. One time in Saint Petersburg, Russia, I was walking down the street with a Russian pastor and another American. Without saying anything we felt that people were staring at us. I asked the pastor if people knew we were not Russians. He replied that no one would mistake us for Russians. He turned to my American friend with his big beard and Russian fur hat, who I thought passed for a Russian, and said that he smiled too much. "Russians do not smile at strangers," we were told. He turned to me and pointed to the gold buttons on my sport jacket and informed me that no Russian men would wear a coat with that kind of flashy buttons. Really, I liked those buttons. When I lived in France, French people did not always know I was an American but they almost always knew I was not French. One time at a market I was asked if I was Polish. I did not know whether to be offended or feel complimented. Some of the strangeness will wear off in time, if you make it through the long uncomfortable process of cultural acclimation. Yet many people will always look at you as a stranger and maybe even consider you a wee bit strange. If you are not prepared for the journey, if you have not had your eyes at least half opened before you left for ministry in another culture, you risk becoming a statistic. You will need to determine the cultural distance you need to cross and the kind of training and pre-field experience you should acquire before attempting to engage in cross-cultural ministry. You will need to get your head out of the clouds, thinking about the adventure and how wonderful it will be once you are there in that special place with those special people who cannot wait to hear you torture their language and offend their sensibilities. You will pass through a thousand language traps, gaffes, and inadvertent cursing before you are able to actually communicate and put two sentences together that are intelligible. In France we had to learn which word to use for "you." Was it the plural form "vous" with my neighbor or "tu" in the singular? Someone explained to me that generally I could use the informal "tu" speaking to children, friends, church members, God, and dogs. "Vous" was the safest to use when first meeting people at the bank, insurance office, government offices, and any other official business. We used "vous" with neighbors until they gave us permission to "tu" them. They even have a verb for that, "tutoyer," rather than the formal "vouvoyer." You might learn things like this through training or through embarrassing correction after you have unwittingly disrespected the mayor or chief of police through inappropriate familiar speech.

It has been reported that one in six missionaries completes only one term of ministry and leaves for reasons which might have been prevented. One of the prime reasons given for attrition is insufficient pre-field preparation.[4] There is an undeniable connection between missionary training and longevity in cross-cultural ministry.[5] William Taylor succinctly states the problem:

> We will never eliminate attrition, whether the expected varieties of retirement, medical return, or the more painful and perhaps preventable varieties. But we attempt to do as much as possible to prevent it, and also are convinced that we can address the issues and process that look primarily at the pre-field phases of missionary preparation and training.[6]

Another study established the following relationship between pre-field training and attrition: "The group of agencies with lowest PAR [preventable attrition rate] had on average 50 percent more training requirements than those with highest attrition of the same agency size group, particularly in the fields of missiology, cross-cultural experience, and missionary training programs."[7] The conclusion was there was less attrition among missionaries who received more training and had more pre-field experience in

---

4. Platt, "Call to Partnership," 196.
5. Blöcher, "Training," 4.
6. Taylor, "Provocative Theme," 69.
7. Blöcher and Lewis, "Further Findings," 114.

ministry.[8] Faithful and fruitful long-term ministry should be one of the primary goals for churches and their missionaries. More attention to preparation for entering another culture might contribute to that becoming a reality.

Cross-cultural workers should be aware of possible causes of attrition and understand why people may resent their presence either as Americans or as missionaries. They must comprehend the deep-seated aversion for any religion other than the dominant religion in some countries or suspicion toward all things religious. They must realize that this suspicion will be doubly true toward those propagating the evangelical faith, often perceived as an American religion or cult. They must be prepared for the possibility that from a human perspective, they may have an unremarkable, imperceptible impact in ministry. They must be willing to ask themselves whether they can serve with joy and satisfaction in the face of formidable challenges, rejection, and spiritual barrenness.

8. Blöcher and Lewis, "Further Findings," 118.

Chapter 1

THEOLOGICAL CONSIDERATIONS

IN PREPARATION FOR CROSS-CULTURAL ministry, there is the hard and humbling work of theological, missiological, and language study. Scripture does not provide a neat, regulated program of training required for missionary candidates. However, there are ministry qualifications which relate to the call and gifting that should be discernible in the lives of those engaged in cross-cultural ministry (1 Tim 3:1–8; Titus 1:5–9).[1] To put it bluntly, churches and mission agencies risk sending out many well-meaning missionaries who are not equipped, gifted, or qualified to plant churches or engage in other areas of cross-cultural ministry. These prospective missionaries may never have been discipled in a church planting atmosphere nor come from churches that have planted other churches. They may never have proven themselves in effective ministry before leaving for another country and culture. They may have insufficient training and experience to be able to organize a church in their own culture much less a foreign culture with the added complexity and complications of life in a strange place. They may have little idea of the challenges of learning a language and adjusting to life in conditions they never imagined. They may align themselves with mission agencies which control rather than coach in order to reproduce clones of North American churches. I have lost count of the number of missionaries who have said to me: "Why didn't anyone tell me what it would be like?" Or, "I wish

1. Davis, "Assessment," 13.

I had received more theological training before I left for the field. I am in way over my head." Or, "I didn't know it would be so hard to learn a language." Yes, many missionaries never plant churches or engage in effective cross-cultural ministry. Part of that responsibility, however, lies at the door of churches and mission agencies who sent them unprepared.

The problem of unprepared missionaries is compounded when churches count on mission agencies for candidate evaluation and the evaluators do not have cross-cultural experience themselves. What happens to these missionaries? Some will last a term and find a reason to leave the field. Of course, there may be legitimate reasons to leave the field after one term, especially if individuals determine that they were mistaken to begin with to have ever undertaken the endeavor. We call that desirable attrition. Yet many others will remain on the field for years, struggling to do ministry with insufficient language skills, with little accountability for how they use their time and resources, with few ideas for outreach and organization, and with no entrance and exit strategy. They may become a missionary-pastor, having followed a missionary-pastor, and will be followed by another missionary-pastor. There may be a small group of believers finally gathered but dependent on the American missionary and money and oblivious to the need of national leadership. The church has little responsibility for the missionary and the missionary has little accountability to the church.

Training of the Twelve and Pauline Mission

The Lord Jesus' training of the Twelve over a span of three years demonstrates the seriousness of intentional preparation for gospel ministry. These men did not receive formal training as we understand and practice it today and certainly did not understand what lay ahead following the death and resurrection of their Savior. Yet in their time with Jesus they were prepared to be sent out to preach the good news of salvation. The Apostle Paul's ministry more specifically addresses the challenges and complexities of cross-cultural ministry with an emphasis on planting churches, yet we will see that there are differences between crossing cultures in the first century and the twenty-first century. Although cross-cultural ministry is in view in this book, this does not imply that cross-cultural ministry alone constitutes true missions. Andreas Köstenberger observes,

> In contemporary usage, missions generally refers to cross-cultural ministry. In biblical terminology, however, it appears that the cross-cultural aspect of Christian ministry is not a necessary part of mission. To be sure, mission may, and frequently will, involve the crossing of ethnic, cultural, or other boundaries, but this is not an integral part of the New Testament concept of mission itself.[2]

The New Testament emphasis is on the task of gospel proclamation, the glorious truth of salvation by grace alone through faith alone in Christ alone. This task leads to planting new communities of baptized believers who identify with the Lord Jesus and continue the work begun two thousand years ago. D. A. Carson understands the training of the twelve disciples as paradigmatic for mission in the church age. He writes concerning the commission of Matthew 10:

> Therefore it is surely not unnatural for Jesus to treat this commission of the Twelve as both an explicit short-term itinerary and a paradigm of the longer mission stretching into the years ahead. For the latter, the Twelve need further instruction beyond those needed for the immediate tour, which they must see as, in part, an exercise anticipating something more. In this sense, the Twelve become a paradigm for other disciples in their post-Pentecost witness, a point Matthew understands (cf. 28:18–20).[3]

We should question whether there is a normative model in Jesus' training of his disciples and whether adopting a supposed model might prevent liberty in adapting training methods to present-day

2. Köstenberger, "Place of Mission," 347–48.
3. Carson, *Matthew*, 242.

needs.[4] The difficulty is amplified by identifying purportedly time-less principles in the training of the Twelve and applying them to the twenty-first century. We then "run the risk of emptying Jesus' mission of its salvation-historical particularity and specificity."[5] The training received by the twelve disciples for their ministry was appropriate for the challenges they were to face. True, not every element of their early commission was retained in the later Matthew 28 commission. Present-day instruction and preparation for mission may differ in many respects. However, thorough training was received by the Twelve. That point must not be lost on those giving or receiving missionary training today.

The life and ministry of the Apostle Paul has long served as an example par excellence of a missionary church planter. Great care must be exercised not to force the apostolic model in all of its details. Since there are no longer apostles today in the strict sense of the word, no one today has the authority for church planting apart from the authority of the local church. Also, it may be debated whether Paul confronted the same cross-cultural challenges in the first century as those faced by missionaries in the twenty-first century. Certainly "the cultural obstacles and spiritual resistance to planting an indigenous church among the Buddhists of Central Thailand or the Uyghur Muslims of N.W. China" differ significantly from the challenges that Paul faced.[6] Nevertheless, the Apostle Paul provides an example of undergoing a lengthy period of training and ministry in spite of his pre-conversion educational achievements.

Approximately fifteen years passed after Paul's conversion on the Damascus Road before the first missionary journey when he began his missionary career of fourteen years. This does not suggest that a specific amount of time should elapse between conversion and vocational ministry. Neither does this suggest that Paul was inactive during that period. During those years in Damascus, Tarsus and vicinity (33–47 or 49 AD), Paul "accumulated his

4. Köstenberger, *Missions of Jesus*, 218.
5. Köstenberger, *Missions of Jesus*, 217.
6. Howell, "Mission in Paul's Epistles," 78.

fundamental experiences."[7] Shortly after his conversion he escaped from Damascus and was engaged in a ministry of proclamation which made him a threat to the religious establishment which needed to be eliminated (Acts 9:22–25). Later he was in Jerusalem "preaching boldly in the name of the Lord" (Acts 9:28). While we do not have a detailed account of his activity before his formal missionary journeys, there are indications that he was active in proclamation and planting churches in Syria and Cilicia (Gal 1:21–23). These churches were visited during a later missionary journey along with Barnabas (Acts 15:23–41). After Barnabas brought Paul back from Tarsus, they were both actively engaged in a teaching ministry in Antioch for a year before being sent out from the church (Acts 11:25–26; 13).

In any case, the commitment to mission preparation seems all the more astounding given that "Paul was not a foreigner to the Greek world. He was a bi-cultural individual, one who was as much at home in the Greek world as he was in the Hebrew world."[8] We should take to heart that "God spent such a long period training one who already knew the Jewish Scriptures so well. This suggests that it is unwise to push young believers too soon into active service, or even into places of responsibility and leadership in a local church or mission."[9] There are obvious and significant differences between bicultural Paul and modern missionaries. The apostle "preached in a world which for the most part had the same culture as that in which he himself had been raised. He did not have to learn other languages but was understood everywhere, and his clothes and customs created no astonishment."[10] In spite of the differences between Paul's first-century ministry and cross-cultural missions in the twenty-first century, we conclude that Paul's training and ministry went hand in hand. We would do well to emulate that model.

7. Hengel and Schwemer, *Paul*, 171.

8. Smalley, "Cultural Implications," 479.

9. Glasser et al., *Crucial Dimensions*, 25.

10. Bavinck, *Science of Missions*, 93.

Ministry Qualifications

The Apostle Paul's frequent exhortations to his coworkers under-line the need for doctrinal and practical thoroughness for the task. Correct doctrine (1 Tim 4:6; 2 Tim 1:13) and evident godliness (1 Tim 3:15; 2 Tim 2:22) are undeniable requisites for all faithful ministers of the gospel and assume a special importance for those ministering in other cultures that provide challenges in a context where the missionary often lacks the support of his faith commu-nity. We find New Testament examples that "all of the men sent out could and did meet the qualifications set forth by Paul in his first letter to Timothy."[11] With the exception of "able to teach" (ESV), most of these traits appear to refer to character qualities, not abili-ties. Many commentators understand "able to teach" demanding "competence and skill in communicating Christian truth."[12] The adjective *didaktikos* might mean "teachable" as well as "able to teach" and seems to refer to "one who pointed out what he knew and admonished his hearers in accord with that knowledge."[13] The Scriptures themselves are the missionary's foundation and final authority "that the man of God may be competent, equipped for every good work" (2 Tim 3:17). Church planters have the privilege and responsibility to entrust to others that which has been com-mitted to them (2 Tim 2:2). The passing of almost two millennia does not diminish the necessity of receiving the training necessary to be competent in the work of the Lord. Teaching and preaching the sacred once-for-all delivered truth of God's Word demands character qualities and competence. These two aspects are not in competition. They are both needed. No ministry should be entered into lightly. Cross-cultural ministry will present unique challenges which will require even more training than that received for min-istry in one's own culture. The mission field has changed. The mis-sion itself and the message have not.

11. Blue, "Theological Training," 175.
12. Lea and Griffin, *1, 2 Timothy*, 111.
13. Quinn and Wacker, *Letters to Timothy*, 258.

Identity and Work of the New Testament Missionary

The definition of mission goes beyond the scope of this study. A few observations, however, are in order. David Bosch, at the beginning of his monumental and influential work on missions, asserts that "since the 1950s there has been a remarkable escalation in the use of the word 'mission' among Christians. This went hand in hand with a significant broadening of the concept, at least in certain circles."[14] This broadening of mission elicited Bishop Stephen Neill's famous warning, "When everything is mission, nothing is mission."[15] Bosch further affirms, "Ultimately, mission remains indefinable. . . . The most we can hope for is to formulate some *approximations* of what mission is all about."[16] I am aware of the debate over the church's mission and frankly do not advocate the expansion and redefinition of mission.[17] In the end, I disagree with Bosch's assessment and the caricature of traditional missionary activity as interested only in saving souls and indifferent to the everyday struggles of people. I would heartily echo Schnabel's conviction in which he identifies mission as *"the activity of a community of faith . . . that is convinced of the truth claims of its faith, and that actively works to win other people to the content of faith and to the way of life of whose truth and necessity the members of that community are convinced"* (emphasis his).[18] Without this conviction, missionaries may lose focus and engage in other activities unconnected to gospel proclamation. We do not need a competitive distinction between ultimate and temporal value of the ministry we do. We do not preach the gospel to the neglect of other needs. We do need, however, to insist on the priority of the gospel to people who will live for all eternity either in the presence of God or banished from it. There is offense in preaching the gospel and opposition to making exclusive claims of salvation in Christ

14. Bosch, *Transforming Mission*, 1.

15. Radner, "Christian Mission," 169n.

16. Bosch, *Transforming Mission*, 9.

17. Leeman et al., *Four Views*; Bevans et al., *Mission of the Church*.

18. Schnabel, *Early Christian Mission*, 11.

alone. Most people will not object to doing good works divorced from the gospel. They may even applaud the good works and those performing them. What many cannot tolerate is gospel-centered and Christ-centered proclamation. Years ago, in a Romanian village, I stood face-to-face with an Orthodox priest and his mob. He ordered us to leave his village. We did not immediately obey him, did all we could to avoid confrontation, and finally left after some heated discussion. We were welcomed in most places when we brought in material aid for people suffering in this postcommunist nation. Our good works rarely offended anyone. Preaching Christ was the stumbling block.

Likewise, the biblical identity and counterpart of the contemporary missionary requires some explanation. Many scholars debate the degree of expectation which Paul had for churches to programmatically participate in missionary work.[19] Bosch, in speaking of first-century churches, suggests that these churches were not "actively involved in direct missionary outreach, but rather that they [were] 'missionary by their very nature,' through their unity, mutual love, exemplary conduct, and radiant joy."[20] In this book, however, I propose the traditional view concerning the continuity of the church's mission engagement in the proclamation of the gospel and the planting of churches. There are clear New Testament exhortations to evangelize and there are good reasons to suppose that the Great Commission was not unfamiliar to Paul.[21] All the evidence points to the conclusion that the "church of the first Christian generation was a genuinely missionary church."[22]

The very use of the word "missionary" remains problematic in mission circles and ministry situations. We might also say that it has been overused. In its etymology, the Latin word *missio* describes the trinitarian teaching regarding the Father sending the Son, and both Father and Son sending the Holy Spirit into the

---

19. Plummer, "Theological Basis," 53.
20. Bosch, *Transforming Mission*, 168.
21. Plummer, "Theological Basis," 269.
22. Neill, *History of Christian Missions*, 22.

world.[23] In the minds of some, the modern usage of the word "mission" is associated with colonialism in the eighteenth and nineteenth centuries, and "missionary" is connected to European institutions and cultural imposition through beliefs and practices contrary to the cultures entered.[24] It has been suggested that the term "missionary" should be dropped since there is no longer an apostolic office.[25] This is wishful thinking. After hundreds of years, there is little reason to think the term will ever drop out of usage. We are left trying to better understand the function of the missionary in our day.

My study of the New Testament and early church practice leads me to identify the work of present-day church planters more closely with a combined understanding of the evangelist and apostle. While we understand that the terminology "missionary" is not found in Scripture, the word does have an etymological relationship to the term "apostle" and it seems likely that New Testament evangelists "carried on the work of the apostles."[26] Ephesians 2:20 indicates that the church is built on the foundation of the apostles. The apostolic office has ceased while "the various functions which they discharged did not lapse with their departure, but continued to be performed by others—notably by the evangelists and the pastors and the teachers."[27] Church history indicates that "in the early church it was thought that the evangelists were those who preached the gospel and were the successors to the apostles in that they laid the foundations of the faith in new areas, appointed shepherds, and then moved to other lands and peoples."[28] The evangelists were active in pioneer regions where the gospel had not yet arrived.[29] In this sense, they resemble present-day missionaries who take the gospel to unreached peoples and regions. For

23. Bosch, *Transforming Mission*, 228.

24. Bosch, *Transforming Mission*, 228.

25. Rowen, "Term Missionary," 97–98.

26. O'Brien, *Letter to the Ephesians*, 299.

27. Bruce, *Epistles*, 347.

28. Hoehner, *Ephesians*, 543.

29. Wood, *Ephesians*, 58.

this reason, the combination term "missionary-evangelist" would be an accurate way to describe present-day missionaries.[30] These observations from the New Testament and early church history should inform our modern practices, especially when we are confronted by mission practices that are unrelated to the first century.

There are only three references to "evangelist" in the New Testament while the verb "to evangelize" occurs dozens of times. Relatively little is known about Philip the evangelist (Acts 21:8). Timothy, a young pastor, is told to do the "work of an evangelist" (2 Tim 4:5). We are left with the one reference by Paul in his epistles to churches (Eph 4:11). These references suggest that originally evangelists, although not apostles in the strict sense of the word, were engaged in preaching the good news. From Ephesians 4:11, we understand that "the apostles and prophets have passed on and their work is now performed by the evangelists and pastor-teachers."[31] From this text, there is a good argument to make that we should understand the New Testament evangelist primarily as a church planter. Evangelists are placed after apostles and prophets and before pastors and teachers. The mission entrusted to the early church "was to see local churches planted in ever increasing numbers all over the known world."[32] It is probable that in their function in the church, evangelists "carried on this foundational work by taking the gospel to new groups of people and 'extended the work of the apostles.'"[33] In the New Testament, evangelism resulted in new believers and the founding of local churches. Anything else is foreign to apostolic practice.[34] We should maintain a distinction between missionaries sent out by churches for a specific task and the obligation to witness incumbent on all believers.[35] This distinction is important to avoid confusion and to preserve the distinctive character of those tasked to take the gospel to the unreached

30. Hesselgrave, *Planting Churches*, 96–98.

31. Campbell, "Work of an Evangelist," 125.

32. Faircloth, *Church Planting*, 19.

33. Combs, "Biblical Role," 38.

34. Combs, "Biblical Role," 28.

35. Bavinck, *Science of Missions*, 68.

or to regions beyond. All Christians are called to be missionaries, or witnesses, in the general sense in which the word is used. Not all Christians are called, equipped, and sent out from their churches with the specific task to plant or to assist in the planting of churches.

On a practical note, we should examine current mission practice. There may be fewer places in the world today that have no gospel witness. We often see, however, the sending of missionaries to places which have been the recipients of decades and even centuries of missionary activity. Should we not have the expectation that where churches have been planted and leaders trained there should be less need for resident missionaries and that at some point even the use of "resident missionaries" is a misnomer? I am reminded of a conversation with an American missionary in a European country. He explained that his father had planted the church and labored there for thirty years. At his father's retirement the son replaced the father as missionary pastor of the church. Churches are free to support this kind of missionary activity. Yet, we should ask ourselves if this kind of ministry is the best use of mission resources and in what way it reflects New Testament missions principles. Now if the father planted the church and in time became pastor, supported by and accountable to the church, I would have no issue with the situation. The question is whether someone is a church-planting missionary who stays in the same church for thirty years and is followed by his son. While I commend them for faithful ministry, I am concerned that this model is foreign to the New Testament.

We see then that there is some divergence in precisely defining the terms "mission" and "missionary." What is more serious is that contemporary and colloquial usage have enlarged their meanings to the point of dilution. They seem to have become catchall words that allow for almost any overseas work or anything vaguely connected with the gospel or geographical displacement to be called missions. As a result, there are "missionaries" who bear little resemblance to their New Testament counterparts. This is not to criticize the good work done or to impugn motives but "crossing geographical boundaries does not, ipso facto, make a person a missionary."[36] When missionaries are engaged in ministry that does not result in planting reproductive fellowships of saved, baptized disciples, then we do well to reevaluate the present situation and return to biblical practices. If everything the church does or should do is mission, "we surrender the distinctive priorities of the Christian mission and risk assignment of the word to the terminological dustbin."[37] Carson relates his experience with groups claiming to do holistic ministry in Chicago with the poor or digging wells in foreign deserts "even though few if any of the workers have taken the time to explain to anyone who Jesus is and what he has done to reconcile us to God. Their ministry isn't holistic. It's halfistic, or quarteristic."[38]

There exists a great need for a clarification of the task of the church. The precise balance might be difficult to achieve between evangelism and good works, between ultimate needs and temporal needs. Thankfully many churches and mission organizations have been able to do both—for example operating hospitals and orphanages—and remain committed to the priority of evangelism and church planting connected with their good works.

> It is not too late for the North American church to reassert that missionaries are sent-out ones—to cast aside the notion that everything is mission and everybody is a missionary, or that the debate is only a semantic one. We believe the future health of the Church and the advancement of the gospel in our own context is directly linked to thinking clearly about the mission task and missionary roles. To go and make disciples of all nations and send out those whom God has called for specific purposes is not only a command, it is the very lifeblood of our task—of advancing the gospel and joining in the work of Jesus to build His global Church.[39]

36. Wagner, *Frontiers*, 76.

37. Hesselgrave, *Communicating Christ*, 3.

38. Carson, "Work for Justice," para. 1.

39. Spitters and Ellison, *When Everything Is Mission*, 80.

Twenty-First-Century Mission

As strange as it may seem, there has been considerable pushback from some evangelicals who are troubled that missionaries continue to be sent to plant churches among different people groups.[40] Perhaps there are legitimate reasons for questioning current and/ or outdated models and methods of church planting and associated mission activity. There is also the need to partner with faithful national churches as much as possible and not compete with them. Yet the task itself cannot be forsaken and missionary-evangelists must still be sent to preach the good news of salvation and to organize local churches. If we follow the apostolic model, we will be persuaded that the missionary task goes beyond preaching the gospel and seeing people come to Christ. Converts are disciples who need to identify with other believers in a local body of Christ.[41] This corporate aspect bears repeating. "Proclaiming the gospel meant for Paul not simply an initial preaching or with it the reaping of converts; it included also a whole range of nurturing and strengthening activities which led to the firm establishment of congregations."[42] This does not minimize the importance of initial evangelism where efforts are made to get the gospel to as many as possible as quickly as possible. Engagement in primary evangelism is essential to the missionary commission. Yet it cannot be the only element. As we see in the New Testament, Paul's gospel proclamation was not complete without an established community of believers.[43]

If, as Carson pointed out earlier, there is something paradigmatic about Jesus' training and sending of the Twelve, how does that apply to the mission of the church today in cross-cultural contexts? Certainly there is a great range of what cross-cultural ministry will look like in different contexts and what training will be needed. We have also witnessed an enlarged sense of mission

40. Engel and Dyrness, *Changing the Mind of Missions*, 151.

41. Köstenberger and O'Brien, *Salvation*, 268–69.

42. O'Brien, *Gospel and Mission*, 43.

43. O'Brien, *Gospel and Mission*, 43.

which includes much that is not even remotely similar to what we learn from the New Testament mission work of the apostles and early churches. This book will not settle the debate on what constitutes mission although there will be discussion later on. My intention is not to diminish the value of anyone's ministry even if I believe some ministry bears little resemblance to the mission as given by Jesus to his disciples and their obedience to that mission. To put it briefly, I would say that if missionary activity lacks the proclamation of the gospel, does not engage in discipleship, and is neither connected to local churches nor involved in some way planting churches, then there is something missing. I recognize the need for creative entry in many places around the world. I understand the necessity of engagement in good works in order to gain access to certain countries or to gain a hearing for the gospel. One missionary friend in an African country started an orphanage as a requirement to work in church planting and pastoral training. If he had gone to Africa to start an orphanage as his primary ministry, then it would be a stretch to call that missions. A good work? Yes, absolutely. Missions? Not in and of itself. There is no mission without the gospel.

So I would simply suggest that biblical missions involves evangelism, discipleship, and the formation of new communities of believers. These efforts will not always be successful or appreciated. Jesus is the Lord of the harvest. New communities of believers will look and function differently in many ways from each other. When it comes to missions we do need to ask some questions. Is digging wells missions? Is literacy training missions? Is poverty relief missions? Is everything churches do and send others to do missions? Or is there something truly distinctive about the Christian message, the Christian mission, and Christian churches? In other words, if something can be accomplished by unbelievers, whether good works or good projects, and there is no advancement of the gospel in any way, then we have seriously strained what constitutes the mission of the church.

Once we have determined the mission of the church, we must determine the kind of training needed to undertake such a weighty task. As we will see there are different components of training. Unless someone sent to minister cross-culturally engages with people cross-culturally before leaving for the field, most of the training received will be theoretical. At the very least there should be serious theological and missiological studies to provide a foundation for ministry and for future learning. Much of what cross-cultural workers need for ministry will not be acquired until they arrive in their place of ministry. But without a solid foundation and significant ministry experience there is the risk of floundering and serious disorientation as the reality of entering another culture and ministering effectively sets in.

There are myriad organizations and individuals which engage in primary evangelism and their efforts are laudable. No one should demean attempts to win as many as possible using whatever legitimate means available to make Christ known. Also, short-term missions have been used of God to create a desire in the hearts of many for full-time engagement in the missionary task. Through them, many hear the gospel for the first time. Yet we should not be satisfied with winning people to Christ in the sense the word "winning" is commonly used. From 1 Corinthians 9:19–23, we understand that winning people to Christ goes beyond the initial conversion experience.[44] We must be persuaded that God's intention in saving people is to gather them into new communities which demonstrate the transforming power and presence of God. These communities point to the ultimate fulfillment of universal peace in the kingdom of God.[45]

In a similar vein, in developing a biblical theology of missions, we conclude from the book of Acts that God established the church as his agency for missions in our era. Wherever the apostles went to preach the gospel it was with the intention to leave churches behind to continue the mission.[46] The call to biblical missions goes beyond seeing people come to Christ. The joy of conversion and sins forgiven is experienced in response to God's offer

44. Köstenberger and O'Brien, *Salvation*, 181.
45. Tiessen, *Reassessing Salvation*, 283.
46. Greenway, *Apostles to the City*, 61.

of grace. Salvation is not simply a one-time experience but results in a new orientation of life as a child of the living God. The gospel which saves sinners is the gospel which sustains the saints. We are called to make disciples who follow in the steps of their Lord and Savior.[47] Cross-cultural ministers of the gospel must be thoroughly equipped to engage in the activity of making disciples which includes providing theological education for future leaders.[48]

My own personal experience and the experiences of many others indicate that cross-cultural ministry will be more demanding and more difficult than in one's own culture. Ministry is never easy and it is not supposed to be. Yet ministry in another culture and in another language compounds the complexity and challenges of ministry. Cross-cultural workers should know that they may never be as effective in a foreign context as in their own country. They may never master the nuances of another language and will struggle to communicate what they really want to say. They may never really feel at home in a strange setting. Yet all is not lost and hopeless. Those who are aware of the challenges and who have diminished expectations will be prepared for the rough road ahead.

47. Peace, "Conflicting Understandings," 9.

48. Sills, *Reaching and Teaching*, 18.

Chapter 2

MISSIOLOGICAL CONSIDERATIONS

IN JANUARY 1988, I went to France with my wife and two children with the intention to plant churches. Before our departure for this adventure, we had founded what many would consider a successful church plant in my hometown of Philadelphia and transitioned the church to new leadership. With a master of divinity degree in hand and domestic church planting experience, I might have been considered an ideal missionary candidate. Yet I was woefully unprepared for the challenges of ministering cross-culturally. I knew little about French history, language, culture, and literature. Later we learned that many French people considered it offensive that historically Christian France was the object of missionary endeavors from, of all places, the United States. Perhaps I should not have been surprised at the reception we received. It was not that people did not like us. Many French people were curious about our presence and we made friends with French neighbors. Our children went to French school and had little French friends. In time, we came to realize that as Baptists we were considered a cult. When we lived in Laon, France, in the late 1980s and early 1990s, the Church of Jesus Christ of the Latter Day Saints (Mormons) rented a property near our house. In the minds of many French people, the only things that distinguished us from Mormons were the white shirts of the young missionaries and some of their taboos. What linked us was our nationality, our accent, and our non-affiliation with the Catholic Church.

Simply put, missionaries are often unaware of the nation's history and religious perspectives or reasons for resistance of the people they seek to reach with the gospel. They do not understand how they will be perceived. They have great difficulty in building bridges and connecting dots to initiate gospel conversation. They have little knowledge of the persons or events which have shaped the nation. They conduct ministry in their new context as they did it in the United States. They may never master the language well enough to effectively communicate on an acceptable level and may have no one to tell them the truth about their lack of language competency. Or, in many cases, they may have had few ministry experiences which prepared them for cross-cultural ministry.

Missiology has been described "as a gadfly in the house of theology, creating unrest and resisting complacency, opposing every ecclesiastical impulse to self-preservation, every desire to stay what we are, every inclination toward provincialism and parochialism."[1] The complexities of cross-cultural ministry demand not only a solid theological foundation and strong convictions but also relational and analytical competence by which one can enter a strange culture and develop an effective strategy for witness. Hence the need for missiological training which should provide tools to understand the sociocultural adequacy of the host culture and to see how God can work with its subideals toward radical transformation at the worldview level. Just as New Testament theology was often developed in missionary encounters with an unbelieving world, so the challenges of ministry in other cultures should always force us to return to Scripture in order that we might see more clearly and speak with greater clarity to the world around us. We need to be reminded that "just as the church ceases to be church when it is not missionary, theology ceases to be theology if it loses its missionary character."[2]

Missiologists have lamented the lack of training that prevented missionaries from understanding their new context and communicating the gospel effectively:

1. Bosch, *Transforming Mission*, 496.
2. Bosch, *Transforming Mission*, 494.

It is increasingly clear that we must master the skill of human exegesis as well as biblical exegesis to meaningfully communicate the gospel in human contexts. We need to study the social, cultural, psychological, and ecological systems in which humans live in order to communicate the gospel in ways the people we serve understand and believe. Requiring only a course or two on human exegesis is like preparing a doctor by teaching him to put on Band-Aids, stitch wounds, and administer artificial resuscitation.[3]

Limitations of Cross-Cultural Training

In the theoretical realm considerable attention has been given to the subject of missionary preparation. A few observations are in order before treating cross-cultural preparation, competencies, and challenges.

First, training alone cannot account for nor guarantee effective ministry. Yet it has been recognized that pre-field training makes a difference in cross-cultural ministry.[4] Second, it must be granted that there are many variables related to personal giftedness, target group receptivity, personality, and expenditure of personal energies. Pre-field training can never anticipate all the challenges and situations that will be faced by church planters. According to research, however, better training would address the majority of reasons for which missionaries leave the field.[5] Third, no amount of pre-field training can completely prepare the prospective missionary for the disorientation and frustrations of cross-cultural ministry. One experienced missionary with graduate missions training recounts that he and his wife were completely unprepared for entrance into another culture and "were blindsided by periods of depression and emotional exhaustion during [their] first four years of Cantonese language study."[6] Fourth, there must be a

3. Hiebert, *Gospel in Human Contexts*, 12–13.

4. Dipple, "Formal and Non-formal," 217.

5. Dipple, "Formal and Non-formal," 217.

6. Commons, "Incarnational Missionary," 17.

willingness to allow for change in the ways cross-cultural church planters are trained. The assumption needs to be challenged that standard and traditional educational approaches are appropriate for our global context.[7] Fifth, the preparation needed by cross-cultural church planters can never be completely furnished by educational institutions or appropriate experiences. Ultimately it will be a question of spiritual resources and Christian character developed by a vital relationship to the living God. Yet the truth of this observation does not permit haphazardness in missionary training approaches. As Bavinck remarks:

> Missionary work is exceedingly exacting and requires deep insight and knowledge. The mistakes made by a missionary are often still visible after centuries. If a missionary has no insight into the society in which he works, and if he has no conception of its religious background, he can commit great errors even with the best of intentions. . . . It is generally recognized today that it is not responsible to send out men who are not prepared for their task.[8]

Cross-Cultural Ministry Preparation

There has been widespread criticism of the practice of sending unqualified individuals to engage in cross-cultural ministry without practical experience or theological training. This practice is unfair to national and newly established churches and has been described as "an act of consummate folly."[9] Acquiring cultural competency is one of the greatest tasks for cross-cultural workers. The cultural distance between the missionary and the respondent culture should in some measure determine the type and amount of prefield cross-cultural training. Degrees of cultural distance are often designated by E-1 (same language, similar cultural heritage), E-2 (new language and some cultural similarity), E-3 (both language

7. Ward, "Educational Preparation," 398.
8. Bavinck, *Science of Missions*, 99.
9. Kane, *Christian World Mission*, 176.

and culture are significantly different).[10] In Winter's opinion, "the highest priority in evangelism today is to develop the cross-cultural knowledge and sensitivities involved in E-2 and E-3 evangelism."[11] It is incumbent on those handling the Word of life and responsible for communicating the good news in another language to another culture that they meet this challenge by giving greater attention to their pre-field preparation. Missionaries need to have the tools to understand "the categories, assumptions, and logic the people use to construct their world."[12] All the tools required cannot be learned in a classroom. However, pre-field preparation should provide them with the tools to be "socialized all over again into a new cultural context."[13]

Importance of Pre-field Preparation

There must be a greater focus on pre-field preparation in order to address the recurring problem of preventable attrition of cross-cultural workers.[14] We need to stress the thoroughness of training commensurate with challenges. This training would include studies in linguistics, anthropology, and strategy in order to be prepared for effective and satisfying long-term ministry.[15] Ministry may not always be fruitful but it should be joyful in spite of difficulties. One of the tragedies I have seen is when missionaries stay on the field because they do not know what they would do if they returned home. I do not want to sound cynical. But they also might enjoy relative financial security from their years of fundraising and building relationships which would be lost if they left their place of ministry. We need to understand that pre-field training provides the ability "to cope reasonably well with early encounters

10. Van Rheenen, *Missions*, 2–3.

11. Winter, "New Macedonia," 349.

12. Hiebert et al., *Folk Religions*, 22.

13. Lingenfelter and Mayers, *Ministering Cross-Culturally*, 23.

14. Taylor, "Provocative Theme," 80.

15. Van Rheenen, "Effective Missionaries," n.p.

in the real world of ministry and set the stage for a pattern of continued learning."[16] We should always be challenging ineffective and outdated missionary preparation and raise the question as to the kind of preparation needed. Radical changes in missionary training have been proposed that do not require relocation to a formal educational setting due to major drawbacks of past trends. One noticeable trend saw the mission movement move "from seeking candidates from Christian schools with a lackluster training in missions, to seeking candidates from secular schools, often with a lackluster preparation for Christian service."[17] Prospective cross-cultural workers need to understand the importance of training that will enable them to effectively communicate the Word of God whenever crossing cultures.[18] They need to take the time to acquire the theological and missiological foundation they will need.

The desire for prospective cross-cultural workers to reach the field quickly is easily understood. There is an uncontainable enthusiasm to engage in "real" ministry. There are thoughts of multitudes without Christ who must hear the good news before it is too late. One might ask: How many are dying without having heard? How many more might have been saved if only they had heard? A passion for souls often provides the rationale for premature departure to the field and the temptation to take shortcuts in pre-field preparation. Some may question taking time for cross-cultural studies when there are open doors for the gospel and ministry opportunities beckon. Some are content to rely on translators rather than take the time and effort to learn another language.[19] Enthusiasm and passion may help someone succeed in getting to the field. Yet when the newness of ministry wanes, the exotic character of overseas living becomes humdrum, and once friendly relationships begin to deteriorate, much more will be needed. We are reminded that "the first ten thousand miles in mission are relatively easy. It is the last eighteen inches that are

16. Ward, "Educational Preparation," 400.
17. Winter, "Eleven Frontiers," 136.
18. Mayers, "Training Missionaries," 308.
19. Steffen, "Missiological Education," 179.

difficult."[20] The sense of urgency is undeniable and admirable, but there must not only be the urgency to go but the willingness to wait and be properly prepared.

Relation to On-Field Training

Both pre-field and on-field training are important components of missionary training. Pre-field training assists in adjusting to a new culture and the disorientation experienced. Research demonstrates, however, that most pre-field training provides simulated and limited experiences in the home culture or through short-term mission trips.[21] Many mission agencies are not equipped to provide extensive on-field training. Further, it may be too much to ask first-term missionaries to not only engage in language studies but also to be involved in further missionary preparation on-field. Also, the question may arise as to the willingness of churches to support missionaries for extended on-field training when they have failed to acquire pre-departure tools. Of course, missionaries should be encouraged to pursue further training. On-field training may be not only appropriate if available, but essential for some missionaries. At issue is the need to acquire adequate pre-field preparation which prepares cross-cultural workers for active and effective ministry without further unnecessary delays once on the field. Churches may have the expectation that those sent abroad are already prepared at some level to engage in on-field ministry following language learning. Where does one find time for on-field training? How many mission agencies are equipped to do on-field training? In an ideal world there may be room for ongoing professional training during the first term and for training facilitators to accomplish this task. In the world of hands-on ministry that becomes difficult. It may be best to pair first-termers with veterans to help in the transition rather than creating a need for more personnel.

20. Hesselgrave, *Today's Choices*, 147.
21. Dooley, "Intercultural Competency," 310.

Need for Specialized Training

The need for specialized training for cross-cultural workers arises in part from the incredible distance between the home culture of the missionary and the host culture. There is an enormous difference between ministering in a culture founded on Christian principles and ministering in a culture where Christianity has not left its marks.[22] An insistence on specialized training, however, risks raising the bar for missionary candidate selection so high that none would qualify. Those risks must be balanced. There is no perfect missionary and we should not insist on unreasonable standards. At the same time, "it would be a grave mistake to suggest that any Tom, Dick, or Harry, without any special training or any particular qualifications, can make an acceptable missionary."[23] We can point to scriptural precedent for specialized missionary training:

> It can be readily seen that Paul, Timothy and Titus were not trained in the same manner as were the saints in Berea, Thessalonica, or any of the other churches which Paul founded. Likewise, the twelve were not trained by our Lord in the same way as were the multitudes. The training of the missionary-evangelist, then, must differ from that of the laity in profundity and intensity in accordance with the gifts which God has given.[24]

Specialized training considers the challenges of ministry to resistant peoples who are defined by the following categories: culturally resistant, theologically resistant, nationally or ethnically resistant and politically resistant. Our urgency to send workers into the harvest cannot override the necessity to send out people as fully prepared as possible.[25] There are skills required for cross-cultural ministry that must be learned. Much of what we learn in order to help us navigate our home culture may provide little help in

---

22. Neill, *Call to Mission*, 95.

23. Kane, *Making of a Missionary*, 60.

24. Hesselgrave, *Planting Churches*, 105.

25. Allison, "Response," 1–2.

another culture.[26] I am a strong advocate of seminary training. Many seminaries provide outstanding training for pastors. Few seminaries, however, have the personnel to provide the training needed for cross-cultural ministry. Before one engages in extensive ministry studies, time should be taken to evaluate the curriculum and the professors. If courses on cross-cultural ministry are not taught by those who have knowledge and experience, it may be necessary to look elsewhere.

Partnership in Pre-field Preparation

Three partners and their roles in pre-field preparation must be considered—the individual called, the local church, and the mission agency. Although these three work together, Scripture clearly demonstrates the primacy of the local church. Mission agencies are subordinate to the ordained sending agency of the local church. When I was missions director of a large church I had a phone conversation with a mission agency executive. He told a missionary from our church, who served halfway around the world, that he could not fellowship with another church of like faith and practice because of different music philosophies. My response to the executive, who had never been involved in cross-cultural ministry, was that our church did not see that as a problem. The missionary was in a country with few solid Bible-believing churches. Positions on issues in the United States were imposed on missionaries who hungered for fellowship with like-minded believers. The missionary did not last long with an agency that sought to control missionaries in areas where there were differences between the church and the agency. If you choose a mission agency apart from your local church, and agencies are often necessary and beneficial, choose carefully.

---

26. Ferris, *Ministry Training*, 2.

Call to Cross-Cultural Ministry

The Apostle Paul had a strong sense of God's calling on his life (Eph 3:8; 1 Tim 2:7). Although few would deny the necessity of a call, the nature of the call to cross-cultural ministry continues to be debated. It has been asserted that in a manner similar to Paul's call to the Gentiles, church planters are called to minister to particular people in a specific place.[27] This is sometimes called a "burden." There may be a kernel of truth to this affirmation when weighed with other factors. The notion of a personal, sometimes mystical call to a particular people, however, often becomes the basis of one's personal decision to become a missionary. When asked to explain the call, one appeals to a subjective experience or a sensation that cannot be described. Churches are then asked to consider missionary support based largely on the person's interpretation of the call received, often without evidence of giftedness or proven experience. Any concept of the call to ministry must not neglect an individual's understanding of what God is doing in his or her life. Yet it must go beyond the individual's understanding to embrace the biblical concept and emphasis of calling. Thus while the call may begin with or include personal recognition of how God is working in one's life, there must be criteria on which to base the reality of that call.

There is considerable difficulty in evaluating the authenticity of God's specific call in a person's life solely in a subjective way. To question that call in someone's life may appear unspiritual. God's call is primarily a call to obedience to his Word as we grow in our understanding of how he has shaped us for ministry.[28] An examination of the call in the New Testament reveals that the "usages of *kaleo*, *klesis*, and *kletos* never represent a person or church as the final agent of the calling of another to serve God. Only God calls someone to ministry, though other persons are normally channels and models of that divine calling."[29] When we look at the

27. Stetzer, *Planting New Churches*, 81.

28. Goff, "Missionary Call," 337.

29. Smallman, *Able to Teach*, 60.

call to mission in narratives in the book of Acts, missionary calls were never separate from the church or other missionaries. The call always involved objective and external elements and was not subjective.[30] It may be that the individualistic nature of American society has some part in the way the missionary call is perceived. The appeal is often made for volunteers for missionary service. From a human perspective volunteerism may have its place. Missionary candidates, however, must recognize the importance of the corporate aspect of the call to missions.[31] An overemphasis on volunteerism may lead to "the sending of many relatively untrained missionaries to accomplish a task which is ill-defined and in which they have not had much experience."[32] The call is related to giftedness. Serving God cross-culturally is not more spiritual than serving God at home. But it is more demanding in some ways and requires different gifts. Those who do not have gifts for cross-cultural ministry should allow God to use them in their own culture rather than seeking to engage in what might be failed and frustrating ministry in another culture.[33]

Another issue related to the call to missions concerns the geographical setting of mission endeavors. In the 1990s, "nine out of ten missionaries were sent out to work among peoples already contacted with the Christian message and, in many cases, already heavily Christian."[34] Perhaps God is calling missionaries to go to the same saturated locations while multitudes are still without a gospel witness.[35] Or it may be that it is time for churches and mission agencies to be more involved in the allocation of missionary personnel rather than accepting at face value an individual call. Certainly this should be done by encouraging, not dictating. Churches and agencies need not stifle initiative and spontaneity. History teaches that "many missionaries have been highly moti-

30. Griffiths, *You and God's Work*, 20.

31. Hesselgrave, *Today's Choices*, 45.

32. Hesselgrave, *Planting Churches*, 99.

33. Wagner, *Frontiers*, 79.

34. Johnson, "It Can Be Done," 43.

35. Johnson, "It Can Be Done," 43.

vated to take risks, to move into uncharted territories, motivated by the conviction of a strong call from God."[36] Yet churches and agencies, led by the Holy Spirit, can provide counsel and direction in order to more equitably distribute the human resources that God brings their way.

Prominence of the Local Church

Acts 13 provides the account of the selection, commissioning, and sending of the first missionaries, Paul and Barnabas. We cannot be absolutely certain how the Holy Spirit directed the church to these men.[37] But there was objective evidence of their capacity to engage in effective ministry. They were specifically chosen from among others while active in observable ministry. The church prayed and fasted. The will of God and the calling of the Holy Spirit upon their lives were confirmed by the church which then commissioned them for ministry. In selecting missionary candidates, the local church must remain God's primary agency for determining the fitness of those who sense a call to cross-cultural ministry. There can be no true call without local church confirmation. The church has the ultimate responsibility "to select, send, and support cross-cultural missionaries, as spiritual gifts are discovered, developed, and deployed."[38] The local church provides a place to gain experience and confirmation of their call.[39] The church as the primary training ground must also provide appropriate ministry opportunities before recommending candidates to mission agencies. The local church must be invested in training prospective missionaries through involvement in various ministries and growth in godliness that is evident to others.[40]

---

36. Pierson, "Lessons in Mission," 75.

37. Polhill, *Acts*, 290.

38. Sawatsky, "Church Planter," 343.

39. Adiwardana, "Formal and Non-formal," 209.

40. Taylor, *Internationalizing Missionary Training*, 6.

Rather than waiting for volunteers, churches should take the initiative to find and encourage those with the required gifts who have proven themselves in ministry.[41] Sadly, many churches leave it to candidates to serve where they choose and receive the training they want before being sent out by a mission agency.[42] The local church should act as the "testing ground of service, a house of prayer, the arena where gifts are confirmed and exercised, the place where leaders and members together evaluate candidates."[43] Historically, there has existed tension between churches and mission agencies which necessitates an integrated model of missions. In reality, churches produce missionaries by providing training, discipling them and evaluating the validity of their missionary call.[44]

Role of Mission Agencies

Mission agencies have become an important partner with local churches in the process of selecting and sending missionaries. These agencies provide a valuable service that most local churches cannot offer to field missionaries. Most mission agencies require their candidates to attend orientation sessions of variable duration. The orientation and training provided by mission agencies greatly varies. It has been observed that this phase of pre-field training could be strengthened if mission agencies and churches worked more closely together to identify areas of emphasis.[45] It should not be expected that mission agencies will fill the gaps in the life of a missionary candidate with a few weeks of training and orientation.[46] Mission agencies cannot provide candidates all the training and experience which they should have received in their local churches and educational institutions. It has not yet been

---

41. Reapsome, "World Evangelization," 119.
42. Sawatsky, "Church Planter," 344.
43. Taylor, "Cross-Cultural Force," 244.
44. Girón, "Integrated Model," 27.
45. Dipple, "Formal and Non-formal," 222.
46. Girón, "Integrated Model," 28.

determined whether the length of the orientation correlates with long-term ministry and prevents attrition.[47] However, mission agencies should consider recent studies dealing with preventable attrition which demonstrate that agencies with higher rates of retention have higher percentages of missionaries with master's and doctoral degrees and require more theological and missiological training.[48] It would be easy and unfair to fault mission agencies for failure in the area of preparing missionaries for the challenges they will face. Yet trainers have observed the following:

> Attendees at missionary orientation courses often seem unable to hear much of what is taught in lectures. . . . However, on their first leave there is often the cry, "We should have been told such and such" about something that had been stressed repeatedly, confirming the suspicion that people who are excitedly preparing for work overseas cannot hear about missionary stress, the cost of adjustment, etc.[49]

Mission agencies do bear some responsibility for the selection process. A local church may select and recommend a prospective missionary candidate to a mission agency. However, once a candidate is approved, the mission agency then makes a recommendation to other churches. Agencies which rely on antiquated or inadequate selection procedures need to review their selection and assessment processes. Personal interviews and letters of reference have not proved to be reliable in selecting missionaries and have little value in the selection process.[50] Mission agencies increasingly rely on psychological testing and screening as one aspect of evaluating prospective missionary candidates.[51] The Minnesota Multiphasic Personality Inventory (MMPI) is now widely used for candidate assessment. At the same time there exists the possibility of the

---

47. Donovan and Myors, "Reflections on Attrition," 57–58.

48. Blöcher, "Training," 2.

49. Donovan and Myors, "Reflections on Attrition," 58.

50. Graham, "How to Select the Best Church Planters," 71.

51. Chira, "Qualitative Survey," 1–2.

misuse of psychological testing.[52] While psychological tests may indicate those who are not qualified, they cannot identify those who will be effective in cross-cultural ministry.[53] Some mission agencies utilize assessment centers to help in the selection and approval process. These centers may be a component of the process. However, "the use of assessment centers is not a panacea that will eliminate all of the problems in selecting missionary candidates. Further, they require considerable effort to perform a careful task analysis and to define candidate characteristics."[54]

Mission agencies may not be equipped to provide training for missionary candidates. It is reasonable to expect that most training has already taken place prior to candidacy or will take place by recommendation of the mission agency. A week or two of orientation may help bond prospective missionaries to the agency and familiarize them with mission policy and procedures. Sessions treating cross-cultural challenges are helpful, especially if taught by experienced individuals. An important role for agencies is to provide direction and encouragement for future missionaries to take the time necessary for further training and internships before approval for field ministry.

Modes of Cross-Cultural Training

There are a number of models which describe various training perspectives. For our purposes the formal, nonformal, and informal models will be considered. According to Thompson, "Christian leaders are formed by God through a variety of experiences including various modes of education: formal, nonformal, and informal."[55] He summarizes the purpose of these different modes of learning: "Each of these learning modes has differing methodologies and goals. The goal of informal learning is acculturation.

52. Chira, "Qualitative Survey," 6.

53. Graham, "How to Select the Best Church Planters," 71.

54. Graham, "How to Select the Best Church Planters," 79.

55. Thompson, "Training Church Planters," 142.

The goal of formal learning is preparation. The goal of nonformal learning is transformation."[56]

Formal Training

Formal learning has been defined "as that form of education that is institutionalized, chronologically graded, and hierarchically structured in a system that spans primary through higher education."[57] This aspect of education is mostly theoretical, leading to a degree or certification and takes place in classrooms with lectures.[58] The vast majority of training in almost half of North American training centers is formal education and evaluators of missionary training are not unanimous on the value of formal training.[59] There are critical concerns related to an overemphasis on formal education to the neglect of other facets. These concerns include a prolonged period of study which diminishes one's ability to learn culture and language, the neglect of character development, and the inadequacy of formal training for cross-cultural work. There is some suspicion that the declining effectiveness of Western mission activity might be connected to the type of formal training received in educational institutions:

> So prolonged and rigorous is the formal enculturation process that the graduate, once the course is finished, finds himself or herself saddled with both family and debt, ensuring postponement of any anticipated venture into missionary work. By the time would-be missionaries from North America arrive at their appointed places of service, they are beyond the age when humans can be expected to learn another language fluently.[60]

56. Thompson, "Competencies," 37.

57. Pazmiño, *Principles and Practices*, 62.

58. Taylor, *Internationalizing Missionary Training*, 7.

59. Windsor, *World Directory*, 4.

60. Bonk, "Between Past and Future," 138.

Formal education has an important place in missionary training. Its importance, however, must neither be underrated nor exaggerated, nor its limitations ignored. One glaring problem is that most theological institutions primarily address accumulating knowledge rather than skills needed for effective ministry in cross-cultural missions.[61] Seminaries normally emphasize training for monocultural ministry and often lack the resources and personnel needed to train for cross-cultural ministry.[62] Educators have observed that "formal education can facilitate a person's development, replace certain deficiencies of environmental experience with a schooled alternative and correct some misunderstandings and misinformation. But it is not of much value in reshaping personality traits and overcoming prejudice."[63] There must be time allotted for serious study. Academic excellence and intellectual achievement should not be denigrated. The demands of cross-cultural ministry require both academic rigor and the giftedness to acquire skills to minister at an acceptable level in another language. If anything, ministry in another culture requires more not less training than ministry in one's own culture.[64]

There may be no agreement on how much formal training is needed or whether an institutional setting will be the best and only option for all candidates. How much formal training one receives will depend on opportunities, motivation, and outside encouragement to pursue the requisite areas of study. As we have seen, missionary training should not be limited to academic achievement.[65] And not all missionary candidates have the same access to or opportunities for formal training. Most nineteenth-century missionaries "were not university trained, but their experience in pioneering situations developed in them scholarly instincts and habits."[66] Experience demonstrates the importance of personal

61. Taylor, *Too Valuable to Lose*, 13.
62. Steffen, "Missiology's Journey," 146.
63. Ward, "Educational Preparation," 404.
64. Griffiths, *You and God's Work*, 13.
65. Girón, "Integrated Model," 31.
66. Ramachandra, *Faiths in Conflict*, 124.

growth after formal education has ended.[67] In other words, more important than academic degrees for cross-cultural ministry is the necessity of being a learner.[68] We also need to counter the perception that missionaries receive mediocre theological training and that practical training is all they need.[69] A missionary with solid theological training has the potential for a greater impact on the field in training leadership for churches.[70] Hiebert warns of the danger of "a theology divorced from human realities and a missiology that lacks theological foundations."[71]

Formal preparation is a piece of the training puzzle that must neither be ignored nor belittled. Yet those who only have formal training may not be as well prepared for cross-cultural ministry as they think. Arriving in another culture with expectations of effective ministry based on the achievements of formal education has often led to disappointment. In summary, formal study is an important component in the educational process. However, "for the missionary to function successfully, so much depends on critical character qualities, attitudes, relational skills, and ability for ministry."[72] These qualities and skills will not be found in a classroom. Hence the need for other modes of training.

Nonformal Training

Nonformal education has been defined "as any organized systematic educational activity carried on outside the framework of the formal system to provide selective types of learning to particular subgroups in the population."[73] Nonformal education would include seminars and small group gatherings for specialized and

67. Kane, *Making of a Missionary*, 61.

68. Harley, *Preparing to Serve*, 66.

69. Blue, "Theological Training," 173.

70. Girón, "Integrated Model," 33.

71. Hiebert, "Missiological Education," 38.

72. Lewis and Ferris, "Outcomes Profile," 41.

73. Pazmiño, *Principles and Practices*, 62.

practical training.[74] Few schools have the ability to integrate formal, nonformal, and informal education.[75] This has led to the establishment of missionary training centers to provide nonformal training which integrates theory and practice and contributes to effective ministry in other cultures.[76] Missionary candidates with Bible training would benefit from the practical training provided by missionary training centers.[77] Nonformal training differs from formal training in seeking to develop competencies needed at each stage of a person's ministry.[78] Those competencies which relate to cross-cultural church planters will be discussed in a later section.

Informal Training

Pazmiño defines informal education as the "lifelong process by which every person acquires and accumulates knowledge, skills, and insights from daily experiences and exposure to the environment and through interactions in life."[79] This type of training is done in community.[80] The importance of practical experience and personal spiritual growth is emphasized for "the acquisition and development of positive and open attitudes toward other cultures, as well as ways of living out our Christianity in a multi-cultural arena."[81] The primary causes of premature field departure are "clustered around issues related to spirituality, character, and relationality in the life of the missionary."[82] Informal training may be the key component missing in missionary preparation and its absence responsible for high rates of attrition. The prospective missionary needs to be provided with real life experience and interaction with

74. Taylor, *Internationalizing Missionary Training*, 7.

75. Taylor, "Cross-Cultural Force," 244.

76. Plueddmann, "Culture, Learning," 229.

77. Ferris and Fuller, "Transforming a Profile," 57.

78. Thompson, "Competencies," 42.

79. Pazmiño, *Principles and Practices*, 62.

80. Taylor, *Internationalizing Missionary Training*, 7.

81. Taylor, *Internationalizing Missionary Training*, 7.

82. Taylor, *Global Missiology*, 489.

others. Informal training reveals areas of weakness and offers an atmosphere for growth.

A comparison between developmental and acquisitional views of learning helps one understand different strengths and emphases; the former places an emphasis on growing and experience; the latter emphasizes teaching and knowledge. An institutional emphasis on acquiring knowledge and earning degrees may unwittingly neglect spiritual formation, character development and practical experience. Informal training which involves gaining experience and promotes spiritual growth complements the academic acquisition of knowledge components.[83]

Dissatisfaction with current missionary training has led to radical proposals such as the suggestion that we abandon the academic model and degree-oriented education.[84] One prominent missiologist related his decision to leave a university setting and stated, "We have grown to believe that we cannot adequately train people for evangelism and church planting within an institutional setting."[85] It is not necessary to agree with dissonant voices, yet their concerns should be heard. Nor should previous comments be interpreted to mean that serious biblical and theological training are unnecessary. The essential and primary nature of these elements in the cross-cultural worker's life and ministry should be evident. They are the foundation on which one builds.

However, the question needs to be asked: What kind of setting will provide the best training? Strengths and advantages of formal training have been acknowledged but there are weaknesses if that is the only training received. There needs to be flexibility in providing biblical and missiological training tailored to the individual and their future ministry.[86] The terms "homoethnic" and "heteroethnic" are used to explain the reality that different kinds of ministry require different training.[87] These terms highlight the

83. Thompson, "Training Church Planters," 43.

84. Ferris, *Renewal in Theological Education*, 16.

85. Van Rheenen, "Change of Life," 7.

86. Taylor, "Cross-Cultural Force," 244.

87. Smallman, *Able to Teach*, 8.

fact that one should not assume that ministry training for and in one's home culture will equip cross-cultural workers for ministry in another culture. For example, pastoral and church planting training by American professors without cross-cultural experience, for ministry in American churches, may not sufficiently prepare someone to plant a church in a cross-cultural context.

Place of Social Sciences

The role of the social sciences and their place in missionary preparation occupy an area of increasing interest to missiologists.[88] We understand, however, that "theological understandings are more fundamental than anthropological ones because they deal with ultimate realities."[89] We must also be aware of the risk of substituting biblical teaching on missions with the social sciences.[90] At the same time we acknowledge the importance of anthropology in order to build relationships and engage in meaningful communication in another culture.[91] As in other areas of mission thinking, we need balance when considering the place of the social sciences in relation to knowledge of the Bible. We want to avoid two extremes. On one hand, knowing much about the Bible and little about culture leads to the "danger of proclaiming a message that is irrelevant and meaningless. On the other hand, if we have an understanding of present-day cultures, but no understanding of the gospel, we have no message to bring."[92] A good argument can be made for the inclusion of the social sciences in missionary preparation:

> The social sciences can also help us understand human change—the factors that influence people's response to the gospel, the methods of evangelism most appropriate in a particular society, and the effects of conversion on the lives and beliefs of new Christians. . . . Too often we

88. Steffen, "Missiological Education," 179.

89. Hiebert, *Cultural Anthropology*, xvi–xvii.

90. Hiebert and Meneses, *Incarnational Ministry*, 367.

91. Hiebert, *Cultural Anthropology*, xx.

92. Hiebert, *Cultural Anthropology*, xx.

equate Christianity with our particular understandings of it and make the gospel captive to our culture. When we see our own cultural biases, we are freed to see the radical, transforming nature of the gospel in a new way.[93]

Missionary candidates who are eager for field ministry face the temptation to give short shrift to studying the social sciences. This is understandable with the limitations of time, energy, and resources.[94] One well-known missiologist confessed the importance of anthropology and regretted that he had no opportunity to study in the field of anthropology before going to the field. He stated, "I myself have often felt that I could have reached that point of effectiveness in two years which took me ten as it was."[95] I would concur with his opinion and share a similar experience. During my first eight years of formal university and graduate studies I never had a course on cultural anthropology. I had virtually no missiological studies during that period. Only years later, after over a decade of cross-cultural ministry, did I have the opportunity and encouragement to pursue further studies in anthropology, contextualization, world religions, and biblical theology of missions. I am convinced that missionaries engaged in communicating the gospel cross-culturally would benefit from anthropological studies in addition to their other training.[96]

> In evangelism and church planting we need to understand the ways people organize their relationships, because these affect profoundly how they make decisions, gather resources, organize activities, marry, rear children, and respond to the gospel. . . . Our ignorance of the social patterns of other communities is a major barrier to planting churches in them.[97]

---

93. Hiebert and Meneses, *Incarnational Ministry*, 369.

94. Ward, "Educational Preparation," 401.

95. Tippett, "Anthropology," 7–8.

96. Tippett, "Anthropology," 16.

97. Hiebert and Meneses, *Incarnational Ministry*, 22.

In concluding this section, it should be evident that missionary training is multifaceted. It is not accomplished in three or thirty years and there is an important caveat. "The notion that we can acquire a body of knowledge that will be valid for our whole existence has itself become a myth. We must learn how to learn, how to select what should be learned, and how to use what has been learned."[98] Formal, informal, and nonformal training should be seen as complementary, not in competition with each other. We should adopt a holistic approach to training that encompasses all three dimensions.[99] Taylor affirms his conviction that we must combine formal, informal, nonformal education "in biblical, theological and cross-cultural studies."[100]

Formal, informal, and nonformal training, essential as they are, cannot in isolation adequately prepare the cross-cultural worker for effective field ministry. As helpful and as necessary classroom work and seminars may be, they must not be considered as separate from practical pre-field ministry experience and evidence of Christian maturity. Three primary areas of missionary training have been identified—"spiritual formation, ministry skills, and an understanding of missiological principles."[101] All three are necessary to be thoroughly equipped for cross-cultural ministry.

There may be the tendency to look at academic achievement as the visible measure of one's readiness for field ministry. I fully support the acquisition of theological knowledge, exegetical skills, and when possible, academic degrees. A bachelor's and master's degree, eight years of formal study in all, prepared me well for pastoral ministry and domestic church planting and less well for cross-cultural ministry. They also provided a solid foundation for future learning. When it came time to study Romanian, I was grateful for having minored in Greek at the university and knowing what case endings were (nominative, genitive, etc.). However,

98. Hiebert, *Cultural Anthropology*, xii.

99. Brynjolfson, "From Synthesis to Synergy," 481.

100. Taylor, *Internationalizing Missionary Training*, 8.

101. Windsor, *World Directory*, 4.

other factors must not be ignored. It may be neither practical nor necessary to require a certain degree as prerequisite for field ministry. Prerequisites for a twenty-three-year-old university graduate may differ markedly from prerequisites for a forty-year-old second careerist with a mature faith whose life skills and church service have molded him for effective ministry in another culture. In all cases there should be adequate theological training, proven effective ministry, and observable character qualities with tailored training in all three areas—formal, informal, nonformal—to fill in gaps perceived by the church and sending agency.

Chapter 3

CROSS-CULTURAL COMPETENCIES

THE NATURE OF THE mission task demands uncovering the challenges and complexity of cross-cultural ministry in the twenty-first century. It may be shocking to discover "that people live not in the same world with different labels attached to it but in radically different conceptual worlds."[1] This reality requires serious preparation which should take into consideration the target nation's religious history, the nature of relations between church and state, and ask important practical questions to provide insight to those who desire to minister in a new cultural context.

Cross-cultural ministry requires the best preparation possible considering one's gifts, experience, and opportunities. Allen J. Thompson's dissertation on church planter competencies provides valuable tools for evaluating prospective church planters. His concern was that some "may be slipping through the selection system with good motives but eventually failing due to a lack of positive match with church planter characteristics."[2] Competencies will not be the same for everyone due to differing gifts, calling, and nature of ministry but are necessary to carry out the call to ministry. There will be some engaged directly in church planting, others in discipleship and evangelism with university students, or ministry among immigrants or refugees. In all cases individuals must understand the context into which they are entering. The

1. Hiebert, *Transforming Worldviews*, 15.
2. Thompson, "Competencies," 5.

words "God called me" have suffered thousands of retractions and explanations when the reality of ministry did not materialize. We often hear testimonies of someone's call to missions, and we rejoice. We then wonder why God only called them for one term on the field. Or why God called them and they never learned the language well enough to communicate at an acceptable level. It has been said there are three reasons given why missionaries leave the field—the reason told the mission agency, the reason the church tells its members, and the real reason.

Contextualization

A detailed definition and discussion of contextualization must be left for another time and the concept is not without controversy. At the same time, its importance cannot be overstated and needs to be briefly addressed with a question. What do cross-cultural workers need to understand in order to build relationships, to initiate gospel encounters, and to establish ministry which can take root in foreign soil? A recent book provides an in-depth and relevant discussion on the dimensions of contextualization from the standpoint that "contextualization is squarely at the intersection of culture, gospel, and gospel bearer."[3] Contextualization as a term and concept has become popular in missiological circles. It has acquired widespread use among many who are concerned with the relationship between Christian faith and culture. The word itself has often been ill-defined, misused, and rightly criticized due to the origin of the term. While the term may be relatively new, the process of contextualization is as old as Christianity itself and a basic principle of God's self-revelation in history and Scripture. My contention is that contextualization, when rightly understood, should be a theological and missiological necessity in all contexts, in all places, for all people.

Contextualization frames the gospel message in communicative forms imbedded in the local language and culture. The gospel

3. Moreau, *Contextualizing the Faith*, vii.

message remains unchanged and leads to planting churches that can flourish in unique sociocultural settings. Certainly there are dangers to uncritical contextualization. Cross-cultural workers must engage in critical and thoughtful application of contextual principles and avoid imposing form and function which are not found in Scripture and which come from their unconsciously contextualized home culture. When we were engaged in planting churches and pastoral training in Romania, a fellow American missionary invited me to visit the church he was planting. He assured me that if I attended a service in his church, I would feel at home as if I were in a church in the United States. How horrible, I thought! What he considered an advantage was in reality a tragedy. Since he did not understand the culture and preached through translators, he planted a church just as he would have in his own country. This mentality needs to die a quick death.

Competencies Defined

Thompson defines a competency as "a quality of a person which results in effective and/or superior performance, which is an underlying characteristic that may be a motive, trait, skill, aspect of one's self-image or social role, or a body of knowledge used."[4] He asks four questions relating to developing church planter training and determining church planter competency.[5]

1. What competencies should a church planter reflect?

2. What knowledge, skills, and attitudes does the learner possess?

3. What "value-added" experiences will help develop the church planter?

4. How will we know when the church planter has changed?

---

4. Thompson, "Competencies," 11.
5. Thompson, "Training Church Planters," 146.

Without questions like these there is little hope of evaluating candidates for mission. Thompson asserts that "a premise in competency-based training is that a learner's current competencies must be identified and compared to the competency profile in order to assess need and design in the learning plan."[6] According to his findings, spiritual life issues were the most important followed by church planter skills and personality.[7] This is an interesting observation since personality is what people find most appealing when measuring a missionary candidate. Personality can also be artificial and distract from a lack of competencies in other areas. Spiritual life issues and ministry skills take more time to develop and to assess. There are candidates who can make a good first impression in their speech and presentation but may not yet have the competencies which really matter. This does not mean that we seek the dullest, plainest, shyest, and least attractive candidates. Good looks and engaging speech are not sinful. They simply should not be determinative without looking at other more important factors.

In another survey, respondents "identified the qualities of perseverance (61 percent), visionary/vision-casting (60 percent), preaching (59 percent), godly and righteous living (58 percent), prayer (56 percent) and evangelism (54 percent) as the most frequently-mentioned competencies for church planter."[8] Effective church planters have been described as "leaders growing spiritually first and foremost, persons with gifting and skills appropriate to the church planting function, and persons with relational personalities whose detrimental rough edges are being honed."[9] The relational aspect becomes especially urgent since it has been observed that many one-term missionaries leave the field due to conflict with other team members.[10] Think about that for a moment. Ambassadors of reconciliation become statistics in attrition because they cannot get along with others. They grow bitter. They

6. Thompson, "Competencies," 51.

7. Thompson, "Competencies," 125.

8. Thompson, "Competencies," 91.

9. Thompson, "Competencies," 126.

10. Keidel, *Conflict or Connection*, 17.

cannot draw from the deep well of forgiveness and extend grace and mercy to others which God has extended to them. Sometimes husbands and wives cannot get along once they are out of their church bubble and safety nets. Usually there were indications that all was not well to begin with but they had the "call" and received the blessing of the church. I have had to intervene in situations where husband and wife could not get along and stayed on the field to save face. They had not been used to spending so much time together when in the United States while they were in school or working. I have lost count of how many couples I have known over almost four decades of ministry who not only left the field but divorced. There are surely times when a missionary team has to break up because of sinful practices and unresolved resentment. There are also times when the devil gets a foothold and works to undermine and eventually destroy the ministry. Missionaries who have never learned how to biblically resolve conflict or who live with unresolved conflict are of little value on the field. They should go home and stay there unless and until they have proven themselves ready to serve again as mature Christians.

An important contribution in the area of church planter profiles and assessment has been made by Charles Ridley. His book, *How to Select Church Planters*, reflects the results of his study of thirteen Protestant denominations. His research led him to develop the following list of thirteen essential qualities of effective church planters: (1) visionizing capacity; (2) intrinsically motivated; (3) creates ownership of ministry; (4) relates to the unchurched; (5) spousal cooperation; (6) effectively builds relationships; (7) committed to church growth; (8) responsive to community; (9) utilizes giftedness of others; (10) flexible and adaptable; (11) builds group cohesiveness; (12) resilience; (13) exercises faith.[11] Although church planters were specifically in mind, these qualities can be generalized for any cross-cultural ministry. Reflection on and discussion of these qualities would be helpful for anyone considering ministry in another culture.

11. Ridley, *Church Planters*, 7–11.

When one understands the importance of adequate training and observable and measurable competencies, we realize that few individuals possess the training and giftedness to effectively work alone. Murray comments that "team ministry may be endorsed primarily for practical reasons, and encouragement may be drawn from New Testament examples of church planting teams, but the theological basis for such teamwork is the teamwork revealed in the doctrine of the Trinity."[12] The New Testament pattern for missionary activity overwhelmingly and indisputably favors the multiplicity of coworkers in mission endeavors—Jesus and the Twelve (Mark 6:7; Luke 10:1), Paul and Barnabas (Acts 13:4), Paul and Silas (Acts 15:40), later joined by Timothy (Acts 16:3) and by Luke (Acts 16:10), Paul accompanied by Priscilla and Aquila (Acts 18:18), Paul sending his assistants Timothy and Erastus ahead of him (Acts 19:22), or later when Paul traveled with others (Acts 20:4).[13] Teamwork is not without its relational challenges as seen in Paul and Barnabas's disagreement over Mark (Acts 15:36–41). Yet as a result, God allowed the church in Antioch to send out two teams of missionaries.[14]

Competencies are not intended to become a human mechanism to evaluate who will succeed in cross-cultural ministry. It should not be expected that similar competencies among church planters will have the same results.[15] Much can be determined through assessments and testing, but until missionaries are engaged in specific ministry and gain experience, it is impossible to gauge their effectiveness.[16] Success as measured by God may be totally different than human measurements. God ultimately is responsible for the field and the harvest and no one is indispensable to the work of God. Your work might fail and shatter. God's work never will.

---

12. Murray, *Church Planting*, 41.

13. Stetzer, *Planting New Churches*, 73.

14. Kistemaker, *Acts*, 570.

15. Thompson, "Competencies," 138.

16. McKaughan, "Missionary Attrition," 15.

Priority of Spiritual Maturity

Churches should encourage excellence in training with an emphasis on spiritual maturity. This training will be intentional, purposeful, and God-honoring. Training must be purposeful in identifying qualities and abilities necessary for spiritual growth and fruitful ministry.[17] Evaluation for ministry must look beyond gifts and skills and place a greater priority on spiritual maturity.[18] We must avoid the mindset that training alone will provide all we need for effective ministry apart from personal spiritual growth in our walk with the Lord.[19] We serve with the conviction that missionary work is ultimately a work of God:

> The principal qualification for ministry, therefore, is not cross-cultural communication skills, effective evangelism technique, professionally implemented church planting strategies, or even strong relational and leadership skills. The principal qualification for missionary service—indeed, for all ministry—is an intimate knowledge of God; without a personal experience of the awe and power of God, all of our professionalism is hollow.[20]

Effective ministry can never be reduced to how much training one receives. All ministry must have its source in a commitment to the Scriptures to shape our lives as disciples of the Lord Jesus.[21] There is the human dimension of training that must not be neglected. There is also the divine dimension which must not be forgotten.

> No deliberate preparation can take the place of the training given by the hand of God in His sovereign dealings with his children long before there is any awareness of His call. Once that call is clear, no gifts can be too valuable, no qualifications too adequate to lay at the feet of

---

17. Ferris, *Ministry Training*, 7.
18. Thompson, "Competencies," 127.
19. Dipple, "Formal and Non-formal," 219.
20. Ferris, *Ministry Training*, vii.
21. Ferris and Lois Fuller, "Transforming a Profile," 50.

Him who loved us and gave Himself for us and for our sins.[22]

In summary, Paul Hiebert, once again drawing from his vast experience, offers this reminder: "The planting and nurturing of churches is first and foremost a spiritual ministry. The evangelist and church planter must begin with a solid theology and ecclesiology and a living faith. He or she calls people to encounter God and to share a spiritual life with one another in a particular church."[23]

Necessity of Experience

When the Holy Spirit called and sent out the first missionaries in Acts 13, he chose men who were actively engaged in effective ministry in their own local church. Why should there be expectations for effective ministry in a cross-cultural context when there has been little or no practical experience in one's local context? I have often been puzzled by prospective missionaries who sense a call to cross-cultural ministry, who live near urban areas with immigrants from their target country, and yet they never engage in ministry with them while still living stateside. They remain in their suburban churches and wait for a send-off to regions beyond to begin their missionary work. In our own multiethnic church in Philadelphia we have several nationalities represented—Kenyan, Cameroonian, South African, Liberian, Dominican, Ecuadoran, Indonesian, etc. A Pew study in 2018 revealed that 15 percent of the population in Philadelphia was foreign-born and had increased 69 percent from 2000–2016.[24] In the ten years we have been here in the city, I have known American missionaries planning to minister overseas in countries from where immigrants have come to live in our city. To my knowledge, we have rarely had anyone come into the city from churches, colleges, or seminaries and ask about serving in a multiethnic church in preparation for cross-cultural

---

22. Houghton, *In Training*, 5.

23. Hiebert and Meneses, *Incarnational Ministry*, 21.

24. Pew, "Philadelphia's Immigrants," 2018.

ministry. During their period of fundraising, many missionary candidates stay safely ensconced in their monocultural, suburban churches and do not venture into the big city to serve in immigrant communities, practice their language skills, or build relationships with strangers. Perhaps no one encouraged them in that direction. Perhaps we failed at recruiting. Wherever the failure lies in requiring experience and acquiring basic cross-cultural insight, the deficiency needs to be addressed by sending churches.

It is widely acknowledged that education and experience are inseparable in missionary formation.[25] If prospective missionaries have given no evidence of ministry competence before departing for the field, why should we expect them to become competent when they land on foreign soil?[26] The following observation is striking and indicative of much current mission practice:

> One of the greatest tragedies I have seen on the mission field is the missionary who has formal theological training, but for all practical purposes is gift-less and has never had any practical ministry before going to the foreign field. These cases invariably demonstrate that the candidating process failed when it did not evaluate the ministry experience of the then-future missionary. The price tag for such cases is terribly high for all involved, for it tends to produce devastating spiritual and emotional defeat.[27]

All the evidence available to us demonstrates that the most effective missionaries have already engaged in effective ministry, and they have the relational skills necessary to build relationships in another culture.[28] Mission candidates and students should be provided with short-term field experience to give them a clearer picture of their gifts and abilities.[29] While director of missions at a church from 1999–2009, I frequently led groups of church

25. Ward, "Educational Preparation," 404.

26. Harley, *Preparing to Serve*, 63–64.

27. Taylor, *Internationalizing Missionary Training*, 5.

28. Girón, "Integrated Model," 34.

29. McKaughan, "Missionary Attrition," 21–22.

members on overseas work and vision trips. This gave those considering cross-cultural ministry an opportunity to test the waters and better understand their own constitutional makeup. Some of them are in cross-cultural ministry today. Others realized that they could best serve God in their own culture. In addition, in order to raise awareness of the needs and challenges in missions, those pursing ministry in missions need to interact with followers of other religions and have opportunities to speak to them of their need of a Savior.[30] This can be accomplished in many diverse urban areas through internships in local churches.

Forty-five years ago a survey of mission executives revealed a consensus concerning "the dilemma of having young people who are very interested in the church planting outreach, but as they get into the work they confess that they do not know how to do it."[31] Decades later we should ask how much has changed. Research indicates that few cross-cultural church planters have any experience planting or assisting in planting churches before leaving for the field; few come from churches engaged in domestic church planting; and few have been discipled "in an atmosphere of church planting."[32] Likewise, Kane launched a twentieth-century challenge that has not lost its value in the twenty-first century:

> Before setting out for distant shores he [the missionary] should have proved himself in church or mission work at home. If he can't win souls in his own culture, what reason is there to believe he will do better in a foreign culture? . . . There should be some evidence of God's blessing in his life and some proof of the power of the Holy Spirit in his ministry before he ventures overseas. Of one thing he can be sure: Success will not come more easily on the mission field.[33]

---

30. Morehead, "Other Religions," 3.

31. Frizen, "Executives," 144.

32. Fisher, "Church-Planting Missionaries," 205–8.

33. Kane, *Making of a Missionary*, 70.

Chapter 4

CROSS-CULTURAL CHALLENGES

WHAT DOES THE HISTORY, culture, and religious climate of a country mean for ministry? I have known missionaries who had such a strong sense of the call of God that they never visited the country where they would serve before moving there. They did not take the time to study and prepare for ministry in a strange place. They had an abundance of zeal but little knowledge or experience. Some survived the disorientation of culture shock experienced upon arrival in a strange place which lacks familiarity.[1] They learned to adapt and engage in ministry. Others experienced culture trauma and became statistics in studies on attrition. Which you become will depend on many factors, not the least of which will be your ability to navigate in a new culture and become bicultural. If you are rigid and unteachable, if you compare everything in your new setting to how good things were in the United States, you will likely become bitter and disgruntled. You may spend more time in lines, more time for paperwork, more time shopping for essentials. You will be frustrated by what you perceive as incompetence or indifference on the part of public servants or store employees toward you. You may be solicited to pay something on the side to expedite the process. Or you may receive special treatment as a foreigner. Your status may get you to the front of the line and you might think you deserve it.

I remember with fondness our time in Romania in the mid-1990s, as well as the irritations at the time and effort needed to

1. Hiebert, *Gospel in Human Contexts*, 21.

accomplish what were simple tasks in the United States. People often asked me the difference between life and ministry in France and Romania. My response was simple. It was much easier to live in France but people were more open to the gospel in Romania. I spent days at the department of motor vehicles jostling with other men to make it to a half-window where I was forced to bend down and stick my big head through the window to address an indifferent official with my limited language skills in a system which knew nothing about efficiency. Even before the office opened, men massed at the outside doors of the building. When the doors opened there was a mad dash down the halls and up the stairs of a once stately, now dilapidated building. The male officials were still using typewriters at that time and employed the hunt-and-peck method of typing. The congestion was such that no women were ever seen there. Some men adopted the tactic of coming with several people to take up more room in the stifling room and shuffle slowly toward the window with all the other sweaty bodies. Waiting in lines at gas stations reminded me of the oil crisis in the United States in the early 1970s. Since we had a car we were able to cross the border into Hungary to shop in the city of Debrecen. The downside was that it took all day with waits of several hours on both sides of the border. With winter coming we had wood delivered in case we were not able to obtain heating oil.

We were not greatly surprised at the difficulties. Before moving to Romania from France, my family drove across Europe twice, once all the way to the Black Sea for "vacation." Driving in other countries presents new challenges and sets of rules and you should learn how to drive a car with a manual transmission. During our first visit to Romania, the lines were so long at the border crossing that I kept the car in neutral with my wife behind the wheel while our young sons and I pushed. We finally crossed the border after midnight with no GPS system on dark narrow roads. We were too tired to continue to our destination and around two o'clock in the morning we stopped at what looked like a hotel. Sensing our desperation, the desk clerk wanted to charge us an exorbitant rate in dollars for a few hours of sleep. We left the hotel and parked on the side of the road until the morning. When we moved to Romania in 1994, we rented a house in the city of Oradea. The house had well water with an intricate system of pumps which frequently broke down. Our plumber would empty out his bag of parts and always seemed to find a way to do repairs. We drank the water for several months before we learned that it was not safe due to the high level of nitrates. Your challenges will be different and you cannot prepare for all of them. You should be prepared in your heart and mind and depend on God's grace to sustain you. Otherwise, you may not make it.

A full explanation of challenges involved in effectively ministering in a cross-cultural setting is beyond the scope of this study. Several areas have been singled out—American identity, religious climate, language acquisition, cultural competency, conscience, and the family—to suggest a starting point for missionary candidates to consider. Yet, there is also the realization that cross-cultural competency, foreign languages, and cultural adjustment cannot be fully learned in a classroom or in a book. Acquiring cross-cultural competency comes through an awareness of the challenges you face and through the experience gained in meeting them. You cannot prepare for all the unknowable situations you will face. Principles must be learned before they can be applied. In short, cross-cultural competency is the work of a lifetime in the place of ministry.

On Being American

Andrew Walls reminds us that "for a good part of the world, to hear the words *American Missions* is to hear first the word *American*."[2] American evangelical missionaries are often baffled by the reception they receive in their place of ministry. This might be especially true if one has had experience in other places that were more welcoming to Americans, to evangelicals, and to missionaries. In some places, being an American might be an advantage. Our family

---

2. Walls, *Missionary Movement*, 222.

personally experienced the difference in reception in places where the descriptors American, evangelical, and missionary posed no difficulty for ministry. For example, in postcommunist Romania in 1994, we were welcomed by Romanians precisely because we were Americans. That we were also evangelical missionaries posed no barrier to building relationships in order to engage in gospel conversation. Romanians were surprised and pleased to meet Americans and openings for the gospel were commonplace. We entered villages where many people had never met an American and certainly not one who spoke their language.

France proved to be less welcoming than other fields of service. Ministry was much more difficult and fruitful gospel encounters were rare. Different histories produce different perspectives and prejudices. In any case, we need to be reminded of an important truth and the attitude we need to have. We must remember that "when we enter another culture, whether across town or across the ocean, we enter as strangers."[3] As strangers, Adeney points to several mistakes Christians commonly make upon entering another culture and offers wise counsel:

> First, although they know they have a lot to learn, they expect to make rapid progress within a few months. In fact, they are less skilled than a child in how to communicate and fit in. . . . If peak efficiency and productivity are your goals, it is probably better not to enter another culture. . . . Secondly, Western Christians think they have a lot to offer. . . . Probably they have more education, more money and more opportunity than many of their national colleagues. That makes them not only rich but also dangerous.[4]

These are wise words and great care must be exercised when you bring your standard of living to another country, especially if your standard of living is way above that of those of your colleagues or the people you are trying to reach. As I mentioned earlier, before we moved from France to Romania in 1994, we had visited the

3. Adeney, *Strange Virtues*, 29.
4. Adeney, *Strange Virtues*, 130–31.

country several times and knew that there was a huge economic disparity between the two countries. We had to exercise more care in how we were perceived. In France I owned a Harley Davidson that I had shipped from the United States. The motorcycle was a curiosity and became a tool for conversation when French people saw and heard it. Yet I knew there was no way I could have a Harley in Romania. Not only would the roads have destroyed it, but it would have been a symbol of luxury attracting unneeded attention and hindering ministry. So I sold it before we left France. As it was, we were targeted as Americans and after two burglaries added two German shepherds to our alarm system and barbed-wire fence.

A Romanian pastor told me to be aware that when many Romanians see an American they see green, that is, the American dollar. This is not a criticism of Romanian people. But we entered an impoverished country which had lived under Communism for decades. People were desperate and most of what they knew about Americans came from television. They thought all Americans were rich. And we were, especially in comparison to most Romanians. Resources can help further ministry or create unhealthy dependency. You must be aware of the economic situation of your place of service. Adeney suggests that "a humble spirit of openness to God and the stranger may be our most valuable asset in a foreign culture."[5] He emphasizes that "if you can handle the stress, your strangerhood becomes a powerful stimulus to understanding yourself, your own culture and the new world presented to your senses."[6]

Religious Commitments

Many Americans are unprepared to enter other cultures which have had a state church, where non-Christian majority religions are in the majority, or where full-blown secularism exists. I do not know if culture shock is greater in entering a nation where the

5. Adeney, *Strange Virtues*, 28.
6. Adeney, *Strange Virtues*, 140.

dominant religion is non-Christian or where religion has been marginalized. In some places you will be surprised by the proliferation of mosques and temples; in others, the absence of religious structures and symbols. When we lived in France I was struck by the absence of evangelical churches in towns and cities. Of course, virtually every town showcased a Catholic church in a conspicuous space in the center square or an elevated setting. Larger cities have impressive and awe-inspiring cathedrals with their towering spires and fearsome gargoyles on the roof edges. The destructive fire at Notre Dame Cathedral in Paris in April 2019 showcased to the world the depth of the roots of Catholicism and its continued influence in a secular society. Unbelievers and believers alike mourned the devastation of this centuries-old symbol and cheered the government's resolution to rebuild it at enormous cost. For many French people, to be French is to be Catholic, and anything else is cultic.

Nonetheless, today the great cathedrals of France are mostly known as tourist attractions. Church attendance on any given Sunday has steadily declined. This decline has been well documented and statistically France has had sharper declines than her European neighbors. After centuries of Christian influence, the rapid dechristianization of France and most of Western Europe has taken place in a relatively short period of time. Dechristianization has been described as the disappearance in the West of a politico-religious system which entailed an obligatory faith for everyone, and practices which, in principle, one must not avoid.[7] Someone going to France from the United States, where Congress opens its sessions with prayer, will be bewildered by the virtual absence of any religious language in political discourse. Most United States presidents, regardless of their political affiliation or religious commitments, close their speeches with some form of "God bless America." I have never heard God's blessing invoked on the French people by a prominent French elected official. Your religious milieu may be different from France but you can be sure that it will also be different than what you have experienced at home. It is a

7. Delumeau, *Christianisme*, 207.

disorienting experience in a strange place when your cultural and religious markers no longer are there to provide a sense of stability and belonging. You will begin to feel your strangerhood and you will feel alone.

In addition, cross-cultural workers must confront the darkness and superstition of the occult which blinds people to spiritual truth. The occult occupies a significant place in France and has grown into a multi-billion dollar business. Each year fifteen million people consult the more than one hundred thousand mediums practicing in France. Sociological research has shown that people no longer have a spiritual compass which religions had provided. In times of crisis, people are looking for certitudes they cannot find in politics or rationality. This reality presents both a challenge and an opportunity for cross-cultural workers. The combat against dark forces cannot be entered without prayer and the power of the Holy Spirit to break the bonds of evil.

The differences between the United States and Europe become clearer through research. In 2005, the Pew Research Center and Council for Foreign Affairs organized a roundtable discussion in connection with the one hundredth anniversary of secularism in France. The topic focused on differences between Europe and the United States in attitudes regarding the place of religion in society. The 2002 Pew Global Attitudes survey was cited to demonstrate "striking differences in public opinion between the U.S. and European countries on issues such as the importance people attach to religion in their lives and the linkage they perceive between belief in God and morality."[8] The majority of Americans consider religion important in their personal lives, associate religion and morality, and do not object to a major role of religion in public life. Europeans place much less importance on religious influence in their lives. Churches in Europe have been in steep decline in numbers and in public influence for many years. The gospel enters these places with great difficulty and humanly insurmountable obstacles.

8. Pew, "Secular Europe and Religious America."

One of the speakers at the event was Peter Berger, professor of sociology and theology at Boston University. He commented on the religious presence in much of the world including the United States and designated Western Europe as the exception in the lack of religious influences. He closed his speech seeking to answer the question of religious perspectives between Europe and the United States. His response is enlightening: "When you deal with historical or social phenomenon of that magnitude, you can be sure of one thing: there's not going to be a single cause. There's going to be a complexity of causes. I've come up with seven. And I'm still not sure."[9] Before seeking to minister in a strange place, you need to explore the religious commitments and understand the reasons for apathy or hostility to the gospel which may be rooted in the country's religious history.

Language Acquisition

For many cross-cultural ministry challenges, there is no training, no counsel, and no warnings which will fully prepare someone for ministry. One of the greatest challenges in adjusting to a new culture is learning a new language and gaining the right to be heard. You can be sure of one thing. The older you are the more difficult it will be to learn a new language. Certainly there are some people who are more gifted than others. But unless you learn a second language at a young age, you will probably never be mistaken for a national. You will make embarrassing mistakes and you might be tempted to limit your interactions with people and confine yourself to safe places. Without a sufficient mastery of the language, however, and without the expansion of a speaker's linguistic and cognitive competency, cross-cultural workers will not be able to understand or engage in complex discussions of issues which concern people. From language gaffes to cultural blunders, much must be learned and experienced firsthand on the ground.

9. Pew, "Secular Europe and Religious America."

It seems uncanny that I remember the mistakes of others better than my own, which are many. When I began studying French in 1988 at the Université de Nancy, I had no idea how difficult it would be. The classes were large with students from around the world. There was no common language of instruction so the teaching was in French from the first day. From what I remember the professor did not even speak English and it would not have helped most students if she did. It was an experience of total immersion. By no means was I equipped after one year of study to preach and teach in French, at least not well enough that anyone would want to listen to me. I will never forget an American studying with me who walked into the cafeteria to order a meal and announced he wanted chicken breast (*sein de poulet*). All the counter workers had a good laugh. I laughed also although I was oblivious to the nature of the fault but glad it was not me who made it. Who would have known that the French speak modestly of chicken chest (*poitrine de poulet*)? Another American missionary cursed from the pulpit for months until a visiting French pastor took him aside and informed him of his foul mouth. The French people in the congregation were either too polite or too embarrassed to tell him. Then there was the missionary who asked for the crow (*corbeau*) to be passed for the offering rather than the basket (*corbeille*). The changing nuances of language are learned only in context. If someone is not ready to be embarrassed or laughed at, they should not attempt to learn and use a foreign language.

A great deal of study has been done on language and how it affects meaning assigned to experience. Disagreement remains between the relation of language and culture, whether viewed simply as a tool for communication or the belief that languages also influence worldview as they "define and guide our perception of experience."[10] Some anthropologists believe "the vocabulary of a language not only reveals what is important to the speakers of a language but also cues the speakers to be more sensitive to the named features of their environment."[11] The complexity of life

10. Robbins, *Cultural Anthropology*, 66.

11. Robbins, *Cultural Anthropology*, 67.

and ministry in cross-cultural contexts requires deep consideration of history, culture, and language. Hiebert in his discussion of worldview affirms the importance of language study. He states, "We must, therefore, study people's language to learn how they see their world. The danger is that we constantly translate their terms into English and in so doing, miss the worldview implicit in their language."[12]

There are no shortcuts to language learning which is often accompanied by tears of frustration. You should be encouraged to know that many will appreciate your attempts to learn their language and will meet your halting phrases with smiles of approval even as you butcher their language. Yet, language skills are the bridge to developing genuine relationships.[13] Michael Griffiths recounts his experience with which many can identify. He states, "In spite of all we heard in training, and despite our having taken a language-learning course with the Summer Institute of Linguistics, nothing had prepared us for the shock of finding ourselves so utterly useless in our ability to evangelize or teach the Bible."[14] The importance of linguistic evaluation of missionary candidates for personnel allocation deserves special attention. Especially important are the linguistic challenges inherent in the language itself and opportunities for programmatic language study. If in fact the clear communication of the gospel is central to the missionary task, then the cross-cultural church planter must obtain language proficiency along with cultural competency.[15]

Language experts have observed that few missionaries become proficient in communicating in a foreign language.[16] I knew an American missionary who went to Western Europe later in life to work in church planting. Someone in his home church in the United States had distant relatives in that country who were encouraged to visit the church. After one visit, they told their

12. Hiebert, *Transforming Worldviews*, 91.

13. Adeney, *Strange Virtues*, 126.

14. Griffiths, "My Pilgrimage," 123.

15. Hesselgrave, *Communicating Christ*, 91.

16. Nida, "Response," 353.

American relative that the missionary's language skills were so poor that they would not be able to listen to him on a regular basis. This scenario is not as uncommon as one might think. In the late 1980s after studying French for only a few months, I realized how easy it was for visitors to be impressed with my command of the French language, a command that was nonexistent. I translated for a pastor who afterward told me how well I spoke French. I knew otherwise and thought to myself, "How do you know? You don't speak French." Without objective, honest, measurable criteria, we can be easily fooled about our language abilities and fool others also.

Observations regarding the study of the biblical languages apply to spoken language study as well. Although university and seminary students do not learn spoken Greek and Hebrew, language study enables them to analyze language structure and introduces them to the complexity of grammar and syntax. The use of the Modern Language Aptitude Test (MLAT) has long been a feature of formal linguistic training. This test serves to measure foreign language learning aptitude. It provides missionary candidates direction in determining how much time to allow for initial language study and the expected degree of difficulty in learning a second language. There are different levels of language difficulty and missionaries should have a realistic perspective of their own language abilities and the time and effort required to learn a new language.[17] Language learning involves understanding, speaking, reading, and writing. Going to the market to buy fruits and vegetables requires basic language skills. Teaching and preaching publicly and communicating the gospel privately require a much higher level of linguistic competence. Missionary candidates might be redirected to fields according to their inherent ability where language structure presents lesser or greater hurdles.[18]

However, when considering three primary aspects of language learning—aptitude, motivation, and opportunity—it must be kept in mind that "aptitude is the least important of the three;

17. Barney and Larson, "Language Problem," 32.

18. Carpenter, "Confessions," 348.

motivation, most important. People with very low aptitude can learn if they are highly motivated."[19] Thus, while the MLAT may be a contributing factor for assessing inherent language learning aptitude, candidates should not be judged or rejected based on aptitude alone.[20]

Missionaries must devote a significant part of their first term to language study. Although most missionaries attend language school, this model of language learning has been criticized. They must understand the limitations of technology in formal language learning and the importance of developing language skills in relationships.[21] There has been a call for the use of nontraditional and nontechnical methods of language learning. Whatever methods or models of language learning are utilized, language theory provides a solid foundation for present and future studies.[22] Of course, one does not learn a new language in four years. It is a lifelong commitment.

Acquiring Cultural Competency

Although I have traveled widely throughout Europe, the Middle East, and Asia for cross-cultural exposure, my cross-cultural ministry experience was primarily in France and Romania. Before we left for France in 1988 it would have been helpful if someone had warned us and informed us of the challenges we would face. Allen Koop provides a sobering analysis of the American contribution to evangelicalism in France between WWII and 1975. Although his observations relate to France, the principles should be taken seriously by anyone seeking to avoid the mistakes of twentieth-century missionaries. American missionaries established a post-war presence in France but were often received unenthusiastically. In addition, many French Protestants took offense at the implication

19. Barney and Larson, "Language Problem," 36.

20. Barney and Larson, "Language Problem," 37.

21. Brewster and Brewster, "Language Learning," 206.

22. Hesselgrave, *Communicating Christ*, 359.

that France was a mission field and saw no need for missionaries.[23] In spite of the dramatic growth of the American evangelical movement in finances and personnel, there was little momentum and scant results. Koop ascribes the minimal impact on French society "not only to the resistance of French culture to their message, but also to the attitudes and policies of the missionaries which led them to separate themselves from the society which they were trying to convert."[24] According to Koop,

> Most missionaries never overcame their linguistic handicap, and many encountered difficulty in adapting to French culture. The concentration of their efforts on the lower middle class, and their reluctance or inability to penetrate the upper and the lower classes, lessened further their influence. . . . The missionaries often imparted the traditions and trappings of midwestern Fundamentalism with little concern for the French religious heritage. American evangelistic strategies pressed for immediate "decisions for Christ," and their church membership policies often insisted upon high standards of social behavior.[25]

American missionaries also learned to their dismay that even in a thoroughly secular society the Catholic Church exercised enormous influence.[26] The lack of outward success took its toll and led to frustration and premature attrition which might have been avoided or reduced if they had been properly prepared.[27] Enthusiasm alone will not sustain someone in the hard challenges and disappointments of cross-cultural ministry. There are reasons to explain indifference and closed doors to the gospel. Knowing them may not change your circumstances, but they might change your attitude and expectations. If your joy depends on reaching your goals or fulfilling your mission agency's expectations of successful

23. Koop, *American Evangelical Missionaries*, 24.

24. Koop, *American Evangelical Missionaries*, 15.

25. Koop, *American Evangelical Missionaries*, 15

26. Koop, *American Evangelical Missionaries*, 23.

27. Koop, *American Evangelical Missionaries*, 166.

ministry, you might want to think twice about packing your bags to leave your country for a strange place.

In this strange place it will help to understand that culture is in many respects a way in which people respond to their environment. This environment does have an important influence on how people learn, think, and on what they value. Although all cultures are fallen and give evidence of rebellion against divine authority, at the same time they are valid, or at least potentially so in some measure, in that they enable people to function within their unique environmental, social, and economic settings. Without cultural training missionaries risk seeing people through their own cultural eyes and coming to the wrong conclusion that all people are basically the same.[28] From ministry experience in postcommunist Romania we learned that many Eastern European Christian women looked aghast at American Christian women who wore makeup and jewelry and did not cover their heads in church services. For five years my wife did not wear jewelry in public and wore head coverings in church. This Eastern European viewpoint was certainly influenced by history and tradition. Just as we would not allow their sensitivities to be imposed on us (although we may voluntarily live under them when ministering in their culture), we must be certain that our culturally influenced sensitivities are not elevated to the place of biblical mandate. We often fail to realize that there is a difference between how we have been programmed through our cultural upbringing and what Scripture explicitly permits, forbids, or commands. Scripture was not given in order to provide a neat and tidy list of every choice with which Christians might be confronted in every cultural setting. We also must apply principles of Scripture and discern its implications for godly living. Contact with other believers and ministry in diverse cultures teaches us that there is both significant overlap and marked continuity in understanding the implications of what constitutes expressions of the Christian life.

Anthropological research and experience show "that systems of belief are eminently reasonable when viewed from within or . . .

28. Van Rheenen, *Missions*, 81.

when we participate in the lives of people who hold those beliefs."[29] An unwillingness or inability to understand these realties from another's perspective leads to frustration, confusion, and discouragement in gospel encounters where a hearing cannot be gained for the gospel. North Americans, due to their relative cultural and linguistic isolation, may be particularly ill-prepared for the shock of ministering in a strange culture with a new language. Ministering cross-culturally demands flexibility regarding cultural norms in communicating the gospel in new relationships with different cultural norms.[30] Missionaries face many issues of conscience and must learn to distinguish between biblical and cultural norms. They must emphasize biblical principles and their application to diverse cultural conventions.[31] In other words, "cultural boundaries must be crossed. Social barriers must be penetrated. Linguistic obstacles must be bridged. Religious resistance must be overcome."[32]

Missionaries face the challenge of relating to three cultures: home culture, host culture, and biblical culture.[33] To understand and navigate these different cultures missionaries "must become adept at differentiating worldview types and diagram how these types influence the target culture. These understandings enable them to communicate God's message so that it interacts with the culture's perspective of reality."[34] Otherwise, they risk irrelevant preaching and teaching which fails to go beyond addressing the initial need for conversion and does not produce strong disciples.[35] We must face the reality that "people in different cultures do not live in the same world with different labels attached to it, but in radically different worlds."[36]

29. Robbins, *Cultural Anthropology*, 15.

30. Dipple, "Formal and Non-formal," 220.

31. Priest, "Missionary Elenctics," 310.

32. Mulholland, "Church for All Peoples," 136.

33. Menconi, "Three Cultures," 519.

34. Van Rheenen, "Missional Helix," n.p.

35. Hiebert et al., *Folk Religions*, 268.

36. Hiebert, "Cultural Differences," 377.

Missionaries often lament the unresponsiveness of those who hear the gospel. Yet we need to consider whether the offense of the gospel or the lack of clarity in communicating it is responsible for the lack of response.[37] In missionary labors "we have to wrestle with the reasons why people reject the gospel, and in particular give due weight to the cultural factors. Some people reject the gospel not because they perceive it to be false, but because they perceive it to be alien."[38] Hiebert succinctly states the problem. "Past missionaries often understood the Scriptures well, but not the people they served. Consequently, their message was often not understood by the people; the churches they planted were often alien and, as a result, remained dependent on outside support for their existence."[39]

Conscience and Culture

When cross-cultural workers enter another culture which has different religious commitments or no religious commitments, they will be confronted with undreamed-of challenges to their own worldview assumptions. They must learn to distinguish between ontological convictions rooted in Scripture and those culture-informed convictions that should not be elevated to the level of scriptural truth. The failure to differentiate between these kinds of conviction will result in what has been called weaker brother missionaries who have strong convictions that they inflict on others without distinguishing transcendent ethical norms from convention and cultural conditioning. There are shared areas of conscience between the messenger of the gospel and the recipients through which the Spirit of God can begin his work of conviction. The missionary risks emphasizing certain areas of conscience informed by cultural variables which find no resonance in the conscience of the receptor. As an example, let us take the issue of

37. Hiebert et al., *Folk Religions*, 20.
38. Hiebert, "Cultural Differences," 24.
39. Hiebert, *Anthropological Reflections*, 10.

the use of alcoholic beverages. Many missionaries sent from the United States have strong convictions about alcohol and their mission agencies require them to be teetotalers. They not only abstain from drinking alcoholic beverages, which is well and good, but they also seek to impose their conviction on others. I am reminded of the time my wife was shopping in our little French town for a gift for her father. The lady in the gift store showed her gadgets and accessories associated with alcohol. My wife explained that her father did not drink alcohol. Another suggestion was made for a gift associated with wine. Again, my wife explained that her father did not drink. The saleslady, clearly exasperated by our lack of sophistication, corrected my wife in telling her that wine is not alcohol. In France and other countries, wine is embedded so deeply into the culture that preaching about abstinence might not be the wisest place to begin or a hobby-horse to ride. Examples could be multiplied in other countries. Of course, you do not need to compromise your strong convictions or personal preferences, but you should be able to distinguish between them. Neither should you expect your convictions and preferences to resonate with others without laying a clear scriptural foundation and allowing the Holy Spirit to transform lives. Just as cultural Gentiles were not required to become cultural Jews in order to convert, we must not present conversion as a break from culture per se but from those elements found in all cultures that are incompatible with kingdom living.

According to Scripture, conscience is a universal, internal faculty (Rom 2:1–15; 2 Cor 4:2; 1 Cor 10:25, 27) that bears witness against us, accusing or excusing us (Rom 2:15), and needs cleansing (Heb 10:22). Our conscience becomes the standard for moral judgment which we use to bear witness to the faults of others. We tend to notice areas of discontinuity where our conscience speaks and where theirs does not or vice-versa. It is at this point that we must be patient and ask for patience, understanding that our conscience has been trained both by the Word of God and by other factors in our spiritual and social environment. There may be some debate as to the relation to conscience as a God-given natural faculty through the created order and how the Holy Spirit works through it. However, it seems clear that unbelievers can have a troubled conscience without a necessary connection to the supernatural activity of the Holy Spirit. Likewise, believers may be troubled in their conscience by behavior for which God does not necessarily condemn them. We understand that conscience is variable (Rom 14; 1 Cor 8; 10:27–32) and a clear conscience does not necessarily guarantee that one has acted correctly.

As believers we do not let conscience be our guide because we understand the decisive role of Scripture in determining our beliefs and practices. What distinguishes conscience is the content, content that is at least in part dependent on cultural norms, ideals, and values. We do not enter the world fully programmed but learn what to do or not to do. This moral programming, a proper activity of society in general and from parents in particular, serves to condone or condemn behavior, to approve or disapprove actions and activities. It may be presumptuous for persons of one culture and tradition, in which they have been acculturated, to dictate the norms for another culture and context when Scripture is silent or not clear. As Robert Priest points out, "Missionaries need to understand the role that culture has played in the formation of their own conscience, and need help in distinguishing scruples grounded in transcendent biblical moral truth from scruples shaped, at least in part, by conventional meaning."[40]

There are at least three ways that we might respond to questionable elements and practices within any culture:

1. Oppose and utterly and immediately reject beliefs or practices that are contrary to Christian and human values (e.g., infanticide, bride-burning);

2. Confront and eventually see diminished or vanished in time those beliefs or practices that are contrary to Scripture (e.g., polygamy, ancestor worship);

3. Retain or transform practices which are valid within a cultural setting and can be used in the service of Christ (e.g., marriage customs, family and holiday traditions).

40. Priest, "Missionary Elenctics," 306.

Likewise, the recognition of differences in the outworking of practical Christian living in diverse cultural contexts does not cause us to abandon all conviction, lacking a specific verse to address an issue. We are not allowed to recklessly and romantically affirm that all is good in other cultures. Yet we may pause before pronouncing a verdict on that which we see only superficially. We should refrain from substituting our signs of sanctification for biblical discipleship. We must depend more on the Holy Spirit to use the Word to guide fellow believers in their faith journey even when their journey does not exactly mirror our own experience.

Importance of the Family

I want to briefly touch on one area that cannot be overemphasized. It is challenging enough to sustain loving and God-honoring family relationships in any place and at any time. In a cross-cultural situation, with the additional stressors of language learning and acclimation to a different context, the challenges will be multiplied. I have personally known families who were committed to cross-cultural missions and did not last long in ministry. There was a dream. There was excitement. There was perhaps a romantic and unrealistic view of cross-cultural ministry. There was naiveté. But there was not unity. I have met couples where one or the other spouse was passionate for cross-cultural ministry. The one-sided enthusiasm was palpable. After years of fundraising, thousands of miles of travel, and great sacrifice they arrived as strangers in a strange place where their communication skills were less than a two-year-old's. The cultural shock led to culture trauma where they were not able and not willing to stay. They longed for home. The truth is that they never should have been there in the first place.

Deep consideration must be given to taking one's family into another culture. This is especially true with children. On one hand, how long will it take to raise the finances needed for passage and ministry for a large family? There are not only the funds needed to support one's growing family. Other issues like schooling, safety, and distance from extended family present challenges. Younger children adapt more easily than teenagers who leave behind friendships established over many years. I have also known couples with large families, who spent years raising funds for ministry abroad, whose primary ministry appeared to be homeschooling their children. Some did not want their children to mix with nationals or avoided the schools because they provided substandard education. On the other hand, how many families have been ruptured by the old colonial model of sending children away to boarding schools? Children are a blessing from the Lord and God can use them to open doors for ministry and friendships with the parents of your children's friends. A balance might be difficult to find, but carelessness in planning is not an option when it comes to family. If couples have never studied, lived, or worked in any place remotely like their prospective place of ministry, it is difficult to bridge the gap between cultures without serious preparation or trial experiences to assess their capacity to live in a different culture, serve in a different language, and rear their children.

Chapter 5

RECOMMENDATIONS

LITTLE HAS BEEN SAID about strategies to reach people with the gospel. The reason is simple. There is no one strategy to employ that will guarantee fruitful ministry. Strategies for evangelism, discipleship, and church planting will not be the same for creative-access nations as for open nations. Methodologies will be different when entering a predominantly Muslim country with restrictions and when entering one with a Christian history and freedom of religion. There are many places where one cannot enter as a missionary-church planter. Yet without a strategy or with flawed strategies the mission enterprise is doomed to failure. A lack of strategy is a major weakness among cross-cultural workers.

> World evangelization has been high on the agendas of churches and missions for over a century now. Most agree upon the urgency of evangelizing the world in the shortest possible time. But, though questions remain as to what world evangelism may mean and entail, the fundamental questions have to do with strategy and method: how best go about this essential task?[1]

There are serious barriers to developing cross-cultural relationships and building bridges for evangelism. Those barriers are even higher when someone enters another culture and is ignorant of the history, the people, their values and traditions, and their religion. I have traveled widely to visit missionaries and am often shocked

1. Weber, "Confronting the World," 87.

71

by the lack of training and experience of those seeking to plant churches cross-culturally. This by no means impugns their integrity. But when we send inexperienced and ill-equipped church planters abroad who have not been taught to think strategically we should not be surprised at the paucity of results in the number of churches actually being planted.

During a visit to Europe several years ago, I met with a missionary who had completed Bible college training in the States, had virtually no stateside church planting experience, and had located his family in a small French town where Catholicism predominated. His strategy was to reach several villages in the region and have people come to his house for Sunday services. Why had no one told him of the futility of such an approach? Why had his mission agency allowed such a venture? After a few years there, with limited language skills, homeschooling his children and with little knowledge of the people, he remained an outsider and is no longer there. He is a good man, a godly individual. Yet he had acquired neither the tools nor the training to do what he believed God had called him to do. What awaited him was frustration and meager results. Later I discovered that few if any of the mission agency's directors had hands-on cross-cultural church planting experience.

After successful language learning, after successful cultural acquisition, and after successful study of history and ministry context, what is next and what is necessary? How do you build relationships with people in another culture, in another language? Bernard Adeney asserts that "friendship is the key to knowledge, communication and wisdom in a foreign context."[2] He explains that "the best way to obtain knowledge in a cross-cultural situation is to make friends with local people."[3] How to make friends will vary in different contexts. Adeney relates the difficulty and frustration experienced by missionaries to Kenya in making African friends. The Americans invited people for meals who either did not show up or did not reciprocate even if they did come. It took an African to explain to them the difference between Kenya and

2. Adeney, *Strange Virtues*, 54.

3. Adeney, *Strange Virtues*, 55.

the West. In much of Africa, invitations are viewed as an obligation and limited to formal occasions. The African way is to simply show up at someone's house unannounced at mealtimes with a small gift. The American couple began stopping by without notice at Kenyan homes and received visits from others. Whether in Africa, Asia, South America, or in Europe, Americans will need the eyes and advice from nationals in order to discover the best way to initiate friendships. Adeney observed that most people upon entering another culture seek out those of their own culture to understand the new context. He warns against the danger of thinking that "cultural skills are theoretical 'facts' that must be understood before they can be applied effectively."[4] He comes to the conclusion that "the most lasting results of your sojourn in another culture are likely to derive from the relationships you make."[5] These relationships will not automatically provide deep understanding into culture. There must be patient and deliberate effort to listen, to study and to comprehend the mental constructs of others. Without these relationships, however, cross-cultural workers will remain adrift and operate out of their own thought processes and backgrounds.

There are two extremes to avoid in preparation for cross-cultural ministry. One extreme is to entertain the idea that profiles, assessments, seminars, and more education will produce effective cross-cultural church planters. What God does through the life of an individual committed to him cannot be adequately measured by human instruments. The work of the Holy Spirit in preparing hearts, both of missionaries and their audience, cannot be reduced to exact calculations and predictions of outcomes. The other extreme is to ignore the importance of learning from past experience and observation and closing one's eyes to the failure of many cross-cultural workers to engage in effective ministry or for church planters to actually plant churches.

The examination of the qualities, gifts and skills of effective missionaries may not provide a precise model that must be strictly applied to all prospective cross-cultural workers. There

4. Adeney, *Strange Virtues*, 49.

5. Adeney, *Strange Virtues*, 57.

may be other reasons for failure or success. However, there ought to be serious consideration of the selection process to ensure that cross-cultural workers have received training appropriate for varied tasks in their field, demonstrate Christian maturity, and have proven themselves before leaving for the field.

Local Church Recommendations

The local church bears ultimate earthly responsibility for the oversight of the missionary enterprise. It may delegate its authority to training institutions and mission agencies. Yet it retains responsibility in the training and selection of missionary candidates. The local church must take seriously its role in providing ministry opportunities to promote the spiritual maturity of those it recommends to cross-cultural ministry. No better place than the local church exists for potential missionary candidates to provide evidence of their gifts and calling. The ministry experience and evaluation of church planters should differ from what is expected more generally of those called to other areas of ministry. Prospective church planter candidates must be directed to engage in those kinds of ministry opportunities that will approximate ministry on the field as closely as possible. They should be nurtured in a church planting atmosphere and engaged at some level in pioneering church planting work. For church planters, this would not necessitate planting a church but at the least would involve working closely in church planting in a pioneer situation.

The local church should be proactive in recruiting those who have proved themselves in effective home ministry before encouraging them to engage in cross-cultural ministry. Research indicates that there should be no expectation of competency on the field if that competency has not been demonstrated at home. We have seen the all-too-common tragedy of churches sending missionaries without first evaluating their ministry experience. This frequently results in spiritual and emotional devastation due to the churches' failure to test them before sending them. In addition, there should be flexibility in helping determine courses of study and needed practical experience for missionary candidates. This would take into consideration the differences between young, inexperienced college and seminary graduates and mature, seasoned second careerists who cannot be expected to return to a traditional setting and start from zero in the educational process.

The local church should exercise oversight in partnership with training institutions and mission agencies in developing a plan for pre-field preparation. This oversight may entail requiring supplemental preparation for unqualified candidates (i.e., seminars, workshops, internships, MLAT) or refusing to support candidates associated with mission agencies with low requirements or inadequate selection procedures. The local church must be willing to take the lead in this oversight and not expect mission agencies to do the work of the local church. Mandatory short- or long-term experiences would allow the local church to better determine the giftedness of prospective candidates.[6] As an example of leadership, local churches could require the MLAT of all prospective candidates who are called to minister in another language. The implementation of this step would not determine whether candidates have been called to the field, but candidates might better understand their aptitude, learning style, and the challenges they will face in language acquisition.[7] The local church must evaluate which agencies should be recommended to church members preparing for cross-cultural ministry. Prospective missionary candidates should be encouraged to enlist with those agencies deemed most competent in the selection process and interested in genuine partnership.

Mission Agency Recommendations

Mission agencies should not be expected to prepare candidates for cross-cultural ministry. The best candidate school of whatever length cannot produce effective cross-cultural workers. Agencies

6. McKaughan, "Missionary Attrition," 21–22.
7. Barney and Larson, "Language Problem," 32.

are partners with local churches, however, in fulfilling the missionary mandate and must give due consideration to the evaluation process. Especially fruitful may be the division of candidate school in two separate sessions, pre-deputation and pre-field. The pre-deputation orientation session would treat mission policy and philosophy, financial concerns, and deputation strategy. At this time the mission agency would evaluate the candidate and propose further culture specific training through seminars and workshops that could be completed during deputation. An internship might be required in the case of those with little practical experience. The pre-field, post-deputation session would provide a second evaluation of the candidate's progress and make further and final recommendations to aid the candidate in preparation for field adjustment.

Research demonstrates that there is often a wide disparity between what mission agencies claim to offer and missionary perception.[8] Those agencies without candidate schools should consider whether their missionaries would benefit from more serious attention to the selection and evaluation process. If agencies do not provide any programmatic pre-field training, the question arises as to how they can properly evaluate prospective candidates and whether local churches should entrust their members to these agencies. Churches and agencies need to work more closely together to address specific areas of frustration identified by field church planters.[9]

Mission agencies should consider testing for language learning aptitude and learning style using the Modern Language Aptitude Test or similar measurement. Even if mission agencies do not use the MLAT for field allocation, candidates might be required to take the test in order to better prepare for language learning challenges and to determine an appropriate learning style. Mission agencies should require candidates to study the religion and history of the people to whom they are sent. Missionaries need to understand the differences between ministry in their culture

8. Davis, "Assessment," 137.

9. Dipple, "Formal and Non-formal," 222.

and ministry in a foreign context. We have seen that missiologists agree that exposure to studies in the social sciences should be expected.[10] Social sciences are not a substitute for a solid theological foundation, but an important and potentially fruitful component for missionary preparation in effectively communicating the gospel.[11]

Mission agencies should consider the adequacy of their formal training requirements. The majority of agencies in one research study make little distinction in training required or provided for church planters compared to cross-cultural workers in other ministries.[12] Training alone does not make leaders but it can "enhance growth in a number of important directions of learning."[13] The rigors and responsibilities of cross-cultural church planting demand a higher level of training than for those engaged in other areas of cross-cultural ministry. Requiring a Master of Divinity degree or its equivalent might not be practical in all cases but should be considered for those directly engaged in planting churches cross-culturally and training leadership for those churches. Mission agencies should also encourage continuing education which contributes to missionary longevity.[14] Continuing education takes on additional importance for those agencies with minimal training expectations.

Mission agencies should consider partnering with other like-minded agencies to provide opportunities for mutually beneficial candidate instruction. Certain agencies have an abundance of resources and a wealth of experience that can be shared. They might also consider using outside training centers (i.e., Summer Institute of Linguistics, Center for Intercultural Training, Mission Training International). These organizations can provide specialized training in areas in which mission agencies lack expertise. A few weeks of concentrated study could make a great difference in the lives

10. Steffen, "Missiological Education," 181.

11. Tippet, "Anthropology," 16.

12. Davis, "Assessment," 138.

13. Thompson, "Competencies," 142.

14. Blöcher, "Training," 2.

and ministries of those who have sufficient theological studies but lack missiological insight.

Mission agencies should require some domestic exposure or experience in church planting for cross-cultural church planters. Vital involvement in a new church plant should be part of pre-field preparation. Why should we expect novice church planters to accomplish under difficult circumstances in the host country what they have not experienced in the home country? Mission agencies should compile a list of required reading for their candidates. In addition to general missions-related reading there should be more reading specifically dealing with cross-cultural challenges. Generally speaking, this could include works by David Bosch, Duane Elmer, David Hesselgrave, Paul Hiebert, Charles Kraft, Craig Ott, Sherwood Lingenfelter, Tom Steffen, Scott Moreau, and Gailyn Van Rheenen, to name a few.

Mission agencies should implement a church planter core competency profile. Many candidates receive no evaluation to determine if they have the requisite gifts and skills for church planting. Thompson lists three essential components: spiritual life dimension, church planting skills, and personal and interpersonal traits.[15] A profile like Thompson's might be constructed to incorporate the qualities and skills suggested by church planters and mission executives. The profile would serve as a mirror to evaluate the candidate and as a map to develop the candidate. Assessment of missionary candidates can also be done following Stetzer's S.H.A.P.E., which evaluates one's spiritual gifts, heart or passion, abilities, personality type, and experiences.[16] Stetzer concludes, "All factors being equal, an assessment assures the selection of better church planters with a higher likelihood of success."[17]

Mission agencies should pay more attention to strategy and evaluation of methodology in planting churches. There are different church planting models for different contexts.[18] However,

15. Thompson, "Competencies," 126.

16. Stetzer, *Planting New Churches*, 78.

17. Stetzer, *Planting New Churches*, 79.

18. Stetzer, *Planting New Churches*, 49.

many missionaries are really "pastoral church planters." This follows from the kind of training they received where a church is not considered planted until the missionary pastor is replaced by a salaried national pastor.[19] While this may be a valid model in rare contexts, other models should be considered. This model owes a great deal to an ecclesiology which requires single pastoral leadership rather than plurality of elders. The practicality of this model is further complicated when newly planted churches have, for all practical purposes, a paid missionary pastor who has settled with wife and family in a locale. When churches are planted by foreigners and dependent on foreign funds for their existence and sustainability, there is little hope for multiplication. More and more church planters realize that a more effective means of planting churches is working from the start, whenever possible, with national workers.

My church planting experiences in France and Romania might not be the same as church planters in other places. At times I was the lead church planting pastor. Other times I was part of a team which included nationals who were in leadership from the beginning. In both countries, churches were planted and matured more quickly when I was not the lead pastor. Rheenen comments that the Apostle Paul "did not initiate one church and become the preaching minister of this church in order to send out others to plant new churches" but rather "saw himself as a church planter working with Timothys and Tituses to initiate and mature new churches."[20] Church planters must be familiar with different church planting models and have the tools for developing a strategy for their situation. An entrance and exit strategy may lead to multiple churches being planted rather than the all-too-common situation of a single church plant dependent on a missionary pastor for its survival. The great need for church planting and the growing world population require training elders as soon as possible and preparing them to serve without the church planter's presence.[21] Church

19. Ott, "Church Planter's Role," 338.

20. Van Rheenen, "Change of Life," 6.

21. Steffen, *Passing the Baton*, 14.

planters must develop a strategy to plant multiple churches and not remain as de facto pastor of one church for years with no end in sight.

Missionary Candidate Recommendations

Neither the ideal candidate nor the ideal course of action in pre-field preparation for cross-cultural ministry exists. The bar should not be raised so high that few qualify. The bar should not be so low that obvious inadequacies are ignored. Cross-cultural workers should be as well-equipped as possible for the task. Pre-field preparation involves not only education but training for a specific task.[22] Missionary candidates need to be assured of the validity of their call to the mission field. Yet what they believe God wants them to do must not be limited to an internal, subjective understanding of that call.[23] Their call requires local church recognition and affirmation of the requisite gifts for cross-cultural ministry. There should also be openness to the place of service consistent with the prayerful, corporate, and strategic mission of the church rather than personal insistence on a limited geographical site.[24]

Missionary candidates should plan their course of pre-field training as early as possible. Theological astuteness needs to be coupled with missiological and relational competence. Once assured of their future place of ministry, in addition to solid theological grounding and standard missiological training, candidates should seek specialized training (religious, linguistic, cultural) that will enable them to minister more effectively on the field and become lifelong learners.[25] Few institutions can provide all the training and insight that need to be acquired prior to field departure. Nor can the classroom prepare someone for all of the challenges to be faced. Yet the expertise and experience of those seasoned

22. Taylor, "Go Adequately Equipped," 37.
23. Griffiths, *You and God's Work*, 20.
24. Johnson, "It Can Be Done," 43.
25. Ward, "Educational Preparation," 400.

by long ministry experience will help sharpen the church planter's tools. Taylor suggests two helpful reminders: (1) "Specific training should be sought to meet specific goals"; and (2) "Seek 'equipping/ training' that will shape you in three areas: character, skills, and knowledge."[26] Time taken for pre-field preparation in these areas may serve both to lengthen ministry and to enable productive ministry.

Missionary candidates should carefully choose a mission agency. It is evident that agency requirements differ significantly and provide different levels of support through their resources. Missionaries may need to enhance their preparation at training centers (SIL, MTI, CIT, Radius International) to acquire skills and training not offered by sending agencies or provided in a traditional educational setting. Missionaries should understand that many agencies may be reluctant to recommend nonaffiliated missionary training schools or seminars. Missionary candidates should, as time and opportunity allow, consider initial engagement in language studies before leaving for the field. Languages will not be sufficiently learned in a classroom.[27] The truth of that assertion does not diminish the importance of pre-field language studies and other factors which must be taken into consideration. It does, however, suggest that missionaries be given a realistic picture of the pitfalls and struggles in learning a new language and have some idea of their own language acquisition abilities. Beginning to understand phonetics, language mechanics, and basic vocabulary will provide a head start on in-depth language learning on the field. Language learning is both frustrating and fulfilling and also a major cause of missionary attrition. Yet fluency in the host language is essential for effective ministry. If the sending agency does not require the MLAT, candidates would do well to be tested in this area in order to discover their learning style and to better prepare them for language acquisition. In my experience, the children of missionaries have invariably learned the language better than their parents. This is to be expected given the way language patterns

26. Taylor, "Go Adequately Equipped," 38.

27. Reed, *Preparing Missionaries*, 66.

and accents are formed and ingrained. In France, people would mistakenly believe our children were French. I was never mistaken for a French person. However, even though adult language learners might never be mistaken for nationals by their speech, they might benefit from language testing before they launch into the endeavor.

Missionary candidates called to plant churches in a cross-cultural context should gain as much church planting experience as possible before leaving for the field. Large urban areas provide opportunities to work with people groups representing countries in which the missionary will be ministering. Missionary candidates would do well to examine the qualities and skills which characterize effective church planters. Special attention should be given to Ridley's essential church planter characteristics. An understanding of these characteristics will enable a prospective church planter to perform a self-evaluation, determine personal strengths and weaknesses, and work to address deficiencies.

CONCLUSION

THERE EXISTS AN UNDENIABLE tension between extensive training which prolongs field departure and inadequate or incomplete training which potentially renders effective, long-term ministry more problematic. Younger candidates are more flexible, struggle less to learn languages, and acclimate more easily to other cultures. Yet advanced studies and experience may provide the foundation for a more stable life and ministry. The added years, however, may contribute to an increased difficulty in language and cultural acquisition. There is also the problem of student debt as a cause for delayed field departure.[1] There is no facile resolution to this tension. Prospective candidates should be evaluated according to the opportunities and experience afforded them in God's design for their lives. There may be the need for greater flexibility in designing appropriate training for cross-cultural workers.

Theological and missiological considerations in extant literature and experience reinforce the importance of pre-field missionary preparation and the necessity of continuing on-field training as one confronts new challenges and adopts new perspectives. There is no one-size-fits-all package that will meet the educational and developmental needs of all cross-cultural missionaries. However, there are identifiable and essential preparatory elements: theological and missiological studies, acquisition of cross-cultural tools, linguistic competency, practical experience, spiritual maturity, and evidence of effective pre-field ministry. These components cannot be neatly organized into a time frame or curriculum. Local churches, led by the Holy Spirit, must exercise their prerogative to select, train, approve, and send those who have first proven

1. Dorr, "Indentured Generation," 13.

themselves. Mission agencies and training institutions, as partners with local churches, can assist missionary candidates in evaluating, providing, and developing the necessary components. Assembling these components does not guarantee successful long-term ministry. But they contribute to one's effectiveness and help prevent premature departure from the field. The bar for prospective missionaries must not be raised impossibly high. Neither must the bar be lowered to accommodate those who sense a call that leads them into hasty and ineffective field ministry. Churches and mission agencies would do well to heed the concern that the uneven, inadequate quality of missionary training is one of the most serious and profound limitations to the cause of missions.[2]

It cannot be denied that many have had effective ministry who had neither the opportunity nor encouragement for adequate pre-field preparation. But the idea should be banished that only minimal training is required if one ministers in primitive societies or among technologically undeveloped peoples. Cross-cultural workers may know more than those to whom they minister, but they must also know the people, their history, their culture, their real and felt needs, their cognitive framework, their kinship relationships, their organizational principles, in short, their way of life, to not only reach them with the gospel but to also disciple them in their context.

There are no shortcuts to acquiring linguistic and cultural competence. The wisdom of sending missionaries to minister in a foreign context, without intensive theological and missiological studies, and with the additional pressures of language acquisition, lifestyle adjustments and child-rearing, must be questioned. Churches and mission agencies, without requiring the impossible and discouraging potential candidates, must establish reasonable standards and expectations for missionary training. At the very least there should be the expectation of significant exposure to the disciplines of a biblical theology of missions, history of missions, studies in world religions and cultural anthropology. There should be evidence of ministry call and effectiveness in the local church

2. Winter, "Re-amateurization of Mission," 4.

before sending people cross-culturally to engage in tasks for which they have shown no aptitude. For those who have not had the benefit of adequate pre-field training, there should be a commitment to continuing training.

One might reasonably ask how old, how long to prepare, how much study? There are no simple answers partly due to the differences in gifts, opportunities, and place of service. The point is that churches and agencies should not be quick in sending missionaries who have not been adequately prepared, who have not begun to develop relational and theological skills and have not demonstrated abilities and effectiveness in the area of their calling. Cross-cultural competency cannot be learned in a classroom. But pre-field training—formal, nonformal, and informal—can help prepare missionaries for the challenges of ministering in another culture and for the culture stress associated with the strangeness of one's new surroundings.

We close with the Christian conviction that the gospel enters this world of religious disenchantment in the person of Jesus Christ. The sacrificial death of Christ provides the only basis for forgiveness and reconciliation for a humanity separated from God. Eckhard J. Schnabel offers these encouraging words applicable to all nations:

> From a human standpoint, the missionary proclamation of the gospel is a communicative impossibility: the message of a crucified Savior is a stumbling block for Jews and nonsense to Gentiles. This is why it is impossible to "force" a decision or to "argue" an unbeliever into the kingdom of God, even if the rhetoric is brilliant and the arguments are theologically compelling—only the power of God can convince people of the truth of the gospel.[3]

Ultimately God is the One who calls and equips his servants. He has given his church a monumental task that involves calling people through the gospel out of the world and into God's marvelous light (Acts 26:18; 1 Pet 2:9). That task continues in establishing local churches for community, discipleship, and in turn continuing

3. Schnabel, *Early Christian Mission*, 1582–83.

the task of proclaiming the gospel of God's grace. We experience joy and privilege as coworkers with God in this task of monumental and eternal significance. As we faithfully plant and water, God will give the increase in his time (1 Cor 3:6–9).

The great need of all people everywhere is to hear the good news of salvation in a resurrected Savior proclaimed prayerfully, boldly, clearly, confidently, compassionately, and patiently. For those engaged in gospel proclamation in any foreign context, all six elements are essential: prayer in intercession for those who need a Savior, boldness through the empowerment of the Holy Spirit, clarity through a mastery of the language and theological concepts, confidence in the power of God to bring new life, compassion toward those who need to hear and see the truth in the lives of those who bear witness to it, and patience for the Lord of the harvest to reap where the gospel has been sown.

The church of Jesus Christ has been entrusted with this calling. May there be every effort to send her best servants well prepared! To him, who has called and empowered his church for this task, be the honor and glory of which he alone is worthy!

BIBLIOGRAPHY

Adeney, Bernard T. *Strange Virtues: Ethics in a Multicultural World*. Downers Grove: InterVarsity, 1995.

Adiwardana, Margaretha. "Formal and Non-formal Pre-field Training: Perspective of the New Sending Countries." In Taylor, *Too Valuable to Lose*, 207–15.

Allison, Norman E. "A Response to 'Training Missionaries to Resistant Peoples.'" Paper presented at the 49th National Conference of the Evangelical Theological Society, Santa Clara, CA, November 20–22, 1997.

Barney, G. Linwood, and Donald N. Larson. "How We Can Lick the Language Problem." *Evangelical Missions Quarterly* 4 (1967) 31–40.

Bavinck, J. H. *An Introduction to the Science of Missions*. Translated by David H. Freeman. Phillipsburg, NJ: Presbyterian & Reformed, 1960.

Bevans, Stephen, et al. *The Mission of the Church: Five Views in Conversation*. Edited by Craig Ott. Grand Rapids: Baker Academic, 2016.

Blöcher, Detlef. "Training Builds Missionaries Up—Lessons from ReMAP II." DMG International. January 22, 2004. https://www.dmgint.de/files/cto_layout/img/red/downloads/PDFs/englisch/missionary_training_s_22104.pdf.

Blöcher, Detlef, and Jonathan Lewis. "Further Findings in the Research Data." In Taylor, *Too Valuable to Lose*, 105–25.

Blue, J. Ronald. "The Necessity of Theological Training for the Missionary." In *Overcoming the World Missions Crisis: Thinking Strategically to Reach the World*, edited by Russell L. Penny, 173–88. Grand Rapids: Kregel, 2001.

Bonk, Jonathan J., ed. *Between Past and Future: Evangelical Mission Entering the Twenty-First Century*. EMS series 10. Pasadena: William Carey, 2003.

Bonk, Jonathan J., ed. "Between Past and Future: Non-Western Theological Education Entering the Twenty-First Century." In Bonk, *Between Past and Future*, 121–46.

Bosch, David J. "An Emerging Paradigm for Mission." *Missiology* 10 (1983) 485–508.

———. *Transforming Mission: Paradigm Shifts in Theology of Mission*. Maryknoll: Orbis, 1991.

Brewster, E. Thomas, and Elizabeth S. Brewster. "Language Learning Midwifery." *Missiology* 8 (1980) 203–9.

Bruce, F. F. *The Epistles to the Colossians, to Philemon, and to the Ephesians.* New International Commentary on the New Testament. Grand Rapids: Eerdmans, 1984.

Brynjolfson, Rob. "From Synthesis to Synergy: The Iguassu Think Tanks." In Taylor, *Global Missiology for the 21st Century*, 477–88.

Campbell, Alastair. "Do the Work of an Evangelist." *Evangelical Quarterly* 64 (1992) 117–29.

Carpenter, John B. "Confessions of a Languagelical Heretic." *Missiology* 24 (1996) 345–50.

Carson, D. A. "How Do We Work for Justice and Not Undermine Evangelism?" *Gospel Coalition*, October 18, 2010. https://www.thegospelcoalition.org/article/asks-carson-justice-evangelism/.

——. *Matthew.* Expositor's Bible Commentary 8. Grand Rapids: Zondervan, 1984.

Chira, Roberta M. "A Qualitative Survey of Current Practices in Missionary Candidate Assessment." PsyD diss., Wheaton College Graduate School, 2002.

Combs, William W. "The Biblical Role of the Evangelist." *Detroit Baptist Seminary Journal* 7 (2002) 23–48.

Commons, Bill. "The Incarnational Missionary." *ABWE Message* 51 (2003) 17.

Cummings, David. "Programmed for Failure—Mission Candidates at Risk." *Evangelical Missions Quarterly* 23 (1987) 240–46.

Davis, Stephen M. "An Assessment of Pre-field Missionary Preparation of Cross-Cultural Church Planters Sent by North American Independent Baptist Churches." DMin / missiology major project, Trinity Evangelical Divinity School, 2004.

Delumeau, Jean. *Le Christianisme Va-t-il Mourir?* Paris: Hachette, 1977.

Dipple, Bruce. "Formal and Non-formal Pre-field Training: Perspective of the Old Sending Countries." In Taylor, *Too Valuable to Lose*, 217–28.

Donovan, Kath, and Ruth Myors. "Reflections on Attrition in Career Missionaries: A Generational Perspective into the Future." In Taylor, *Too Valuable to Lose*, 41–73.

Dooley, Marianna H. "Intercultural Competency in Relation to Missionary Effectiveness: Implications for On-Field Training." PhD diss., Trinity Evangelical Divinity School, 1998.

Dorr, Linda. "Release the Indentured Generation!" *Mission Frontiers* 26 (2004) 11–13.

Elmer, Duane. *Cross-Cultural Conflict: Building Relationships for Effective Ministry.* Downers Grove: InterVarsity, 1993.

——. *Cross-Cultural Connections: Stepping Out and Fitting In Around the World.* Downers Grove: InterVarsity, 2002.

Engel, James F., and William A. Dyrness. *Changing the Mind of Missions: Where Have We Gone Wrong?* Downers Grove: InterVarsity, 2000.

Escobar, Samuel. *The New Global Mission: The Gospel from Everywhere to Everyone.* Christian Doctrine in Global Perspective. Downers Grove: InterVarsity, 2003.

Faircloth, Samuel D. *Church Planting for Reproduction*. Grand Rapids: Baker, 1991.

Ferris, Robert W., ed. *Establishing Ministry Training: A Manual for Programme Developers*. Pasadena: William Carey, 1995.

———. *Renewal in Theological Education: Strategies for Change*. Wheaton, IL: Billy Graham Center, 1990.

Ferris, Robert W., and Lois Fuller. "Transforming a Profile into Training Goals." In *Establishing Ministry Training: A Manual for Programme Developers*, 43–64. Pasadena: William Carey, 1995.

Fisher, Ron. "Why Don't We Have More Church-Planting Missionaries?" *Evangelical Missions Quarterly* 14 (1978) 205–11.

Frizen, Edwin L. "Executives Tell Missions Profs What They Think." *Evangelical Missions Quarterly* 8 (1972) 143–47.

Girón, Rodolfo. "An Integrated Model of Missions." In Taylor, *Too Valuable to Lose*, 25–40.

Glasser, Arthur F., et al. *Crucial Dimensions in World Evangelization*. Pasadena: William Carey, 1976.

Goff, William E. "Missionary Call and Service." In *Missiology: An Introduction to the Foundations, History, and Strategies of World Missions*, edited by John Mark Terry et al., 334–46. Nashville: Broadman & Holman, 1998.

Graham, Thomas. "How to Select the Best Church Planters." *Evangelical Missions Quarterly* 23 (1987) 70–79.

Greenway, Roger S. *Apostles to the City: Biblical Strategies for Urban Missions*. Grand Rapids: Baker, 1978.

Griffiths, Michael C. *You and God's Work Overseas*. Chicago: InterVarsity, 1967.

———. "My Pilgrimage in Mission." *International Bulletin of Missionary Research* 28 (2004) 122–25.

Harley, David. *Preparing to Serve: Training for Cross-Cultural Mission*. Pasadena: William Carey, 1995.

Hengel, Martin, and Anna Maria Schwemer. *Paul between Damascus and Antioch: The Unknown Years*. Translated by John Bowden. Louisville: Westminster John Knox, 1997.

Hesselgrave, David J. *Communicating Christ Cross-Culturally: An Introduction to Missionary Communication*. 2nd ed. Grand Rapids: Zondervan, 1991.

———. "Evangelical Mission in 2001 and Beyond—Who Will Set the Agenda?" *Trinity World Forum*, Spring 2001.

———. *Planting Churches Cross-Culturally: North America and Beyond*. 2nd ed. Grand Rapids: Baker Academic, 2000.

———. *Today's Choices for Tomorrow's Mission*. Grand Rapids: Zondervan, 1988.

Hiebert, Paul G. *Anthropological Reflections on Missiological Issues*. Grand Rapids: Baker Academic, 1994.

———. *Cultural Anthropology*. Grand Rapids: Baker Academic, 1983.

———. "Cultural Differences and the Communication of the Gospel." In Winter and Hawthorne, *Perspectives on the World Christian Movement*, 373–83.

———. *The Gospel in Human Contexts: Anthropological Explorations for Contemporary Missions.* Grand Rapids: Baker Academic, 2009.

———. "Missiological Education for a Global Era." In *Missiological Education for the 21st Century*, edited by J. Dudley Woodberry et al., 34–42. Maryknoll: Orbis, 1996.

Hiebert, Paul G., and Eloise Hiebert Meneses. *Incarnational Ministry: Planting Churches in Band, Tribal, Peasant, and Urban Societies.* Grand Rapids: Baker Academic, 1995.

Hiebert, Paul, et al. *Understanding Folk Religions: A Christian Response to Popular Beliefs and Practices.* Grand Rapids: Baker Academic, 1999.

Hoehner, Howard W. *Ephesians: An Exegetical Commentary.* Grand Rapids: Baker Academic, 2002.

Houghton, A. T., ed. *In Training: A Guide to the Preparation of the Missionary Based on Material Left by Rowland Hogben.* Chicago: InterVarsity, 1946.

Howell, Don N., Jr. "Mission in Paul's Epistles: Genesis, Patterns, and Dynamics." In *Mission in the New Testament: An Evangelical Approach*, edited by William J. Larkin Jr. and Joel F. Williams, 63–91. Maryknoll: Orbis, 1999.

Johnson, Todd M. "'It Can Be Done': The Impact of Modernity and Postmodernity on the Global Mission Plans of Churches and Agencies." In Bonk, *Between Past and Future*, 37–49.

Kane, J. Herbert. *A Concise History of the Christian World Mission.* Grand Rapids: Baker Academic, 1982.

———. *The Making of a Missionary.* 2nd ed. Grand Rapids: Baker, 1975.

Keidel, Levi. *Conflict or Connection: Interpersonal Relationships in Cross-Cultural Settings.* Carol Stream, IL: Evangelical Missions Information Service, 1996.

Kirby, Jon P. "Language and Culture Learning *Is* Conversion . . . *Is* Ministry." *Missiology* 23 (1995) 131–43.

Kistemaker, Simon J. *Acts: New Testament Commentary.* Grand Rapids: Baker, 1990.

Koop, Allen V. *American Evangelical Missionaries in France, 1945–1975.* Latham, MD: University Press of America, 1986.

Köstenberger, Andreas J. *The Missions of Jesus and the Disciples: With Implications for the Fourth Gospel's Purpose and the Mission of the Contemporary Church.* Grand Rapids: Eerdmans, 1998.

———. "The Place of Mission in New Testament Theology." *Missiology* 27 (1999) 347–62.

Köstenberger, Andreas J., and Peter T. O'Brien. *Salvation to the Ends of the Earth: A Biblical Theology of Missions.* Downers Grove: InterVarsity, 2001.

Larson, Donald N. "Linguistic and Sociolinguistic Factors in Missionary Allocation." *Evangelical Missions Quarterly* 9 (1973) 74–84.

Lea, Thomas D., and Hayne P. Griffin Jr. *1, 2 Timothy, Titus.* New American Commentary 34. Nashville: Broadman, 1992.

BIBLIOGRAPHY

Leeman, Jonathan, et al. *Four Views on the Church's Mission*. Edited by Jason S. Sexton. Grand Rapids: Zondervan, 2017.

Lewis, Jonathan, and Robert Ferris. "Developing an Outcomes Profile." In *Establishing Ministry Training: A Manual for Programme Developers*. Pasadena: William Carey, 1995.

Lingenfelter, Sherwood. *Agents of Transformation: A Guide for Effective Cross-Cultural Ministry*. Grand Rapids: Baker Academic, 1996.

———. *Transforming Culture: A Challenge for Christian Mission*. Grand Rapids: Baker Academic, 1992.

Lingenfelter, Sherwood G., and Marvin K. Mayers. *Ministering Cross-Culturally: An Incarnational Model for Personal Relationships*. Grand Rapids: Baker Academic, 1986.

MacArthur, John, Jr. *I Timothy*. MacArthur New Testament Commentary. Chicago: Moody, 1995.

Marshall, I. Howard. *The Pastoral Epistles*. International Critical Commentary. Edited by J. A. Emerton. Edinburgh: T. & T. Clark, 1999.

Mayers, Marvin K. "Training Missionaries for the 21st Century." *Evangelical Missions Quarterly* 22 (1985) 306–12.

McKaughan, Paul. "Missionary Attrition: Defining the Problem." In Taylor, *Too Valuable to Lose*, 15–24.

Menconi, Margo Lyn. "Understanding and Relating to the Three Cultures of Cross-Cultural Ministry in Russia." *Missiology* 24 (1996) 519–31.

Moreau, A. Scott. *Contextualizing the Faith: A Holistic Approach*. Grand Rapids: Baker Academic, 2018.

Morehead, John W. "Other Religions and New Religions Are Also a Mission Challenge." *Occasional Bulletin of the Evangelical Missiology Society* 15 (2003) 3–5.

Mulholland, Kenneth B. "A Church for All Peoples." In Winter and Hawthorne, *Perspectives on the World Christian Movement*, 135–36.

Murray, Stuart. *Church Planting: Laying Foundations*. Scottdale, PA: Herald, 2001.

Neill, Stephen Charles. *Call to Mission*. Philadelphia: Fortress, 1970.

———. *A History of Christian Missions*. New York: Penguin, 1990.

Nida, Eugene A. "Why Confess? A Response to John B. Carpenter." *Missiology* 24 (1996) 351–53.

O'Brien, Peter T. *Gospel and Mission in the Writings of Paul: An Exegetical and Theological Analysis*. Grand Rapids: Baker Academic, 1995.

———. *The Letter to the Ephesians*. Pillar New Testament Commentary. Grand Rapids: Eerdmans, 1999.

Ott, Craig. "Matching the Church Planter's Role with the Church Planting Model." *Evangelical Missions Quarterly* 37 (2001) 338–44.

Pazmiño, Robert W. *Principles and Practices of Christian Education: An Evangelical Perspective*. Grand Rapids: Baker, 1992.

Peace, Richard V. "Conflicting Understandings of Christian Conversion: A Missiological Challenge." *International Bulletin of Missionary Research* 28 (2004) 8–14.

Pew Research Center. "Philadelphia's Immigrants: Who They Are and How They Are Changing the City." Pew. June 7, 2018. https://www.pewtrusts.org/ research-and-analysis/reports/2018/06/07/philadelphias-immigrants.

———. "Secular Europe and Religious America: Implications for Transatlantic Relations." Pew. April 21, 2005. http://www.pewforum.org/2005/04/21/ secular-europe-and-religious-america-implications-for-transatlantic-relations/.

Pierson, Paul E. "Lessons in Mission from the Twentieth Century: Conciliar Missions." In Bonk, *Between Past and Future*, 67–84.

Platt, Daryl. "A Call to Partnership in the Missionary Selection Process." In Taylor, *Too Valuable to Lose*, 195–206.

Plueddmann, James E. "Culture, Learning and Missionary Training." In Taylor, *Internationalizing Missionary Training*, 217–30.

Plummer, Robert L. "A Theological Basis for the Church's Mission in Paul." *Westminster Theological Journal* 64 (2002) 253–71.

Polhill, John B. *Acts*. New American Commentary 26. Nashville: Broadman, 1992.

Priest, Robert J. "Cultural Anthropology, Sin, and the Missionary." In *God and Culture: Essays in Honor of Carl F. H. Henry*, edited by D. A. Carson and John D. Woodbridge, 85–105. Grand Rapids: Eerdmans, 1993.

———. "Missionary Elenctics: Conscience and Culture." *Missiology* 22 (1994) 291–315.

Quinn, Jerome D., and William C. Wacker. *The First and Second Letters to Timothy: A New Translation with Notes and Commentary*. Grand Rapids: Eerdmans, 2000.

Radner, Ephraim. "Christian Mission and the Lambeth Conferences." In *The Lambeth Conference: Theology, History, Polity and Purpose*, edited by Paul Avis and Benjamin M. Guyer, 132–72. London: Bloomsbury T. & T. Clark, 2017.

Ramachandra, Vinoth. *Faiths in Conflict: Christian Integrity in a Multicultural World*. Downers Grove: InterVarsity, 1999.

Reapsome, Jim. "What's Holding Up World Evangelization? Strategic Hurdles." *Evangelical Missions Quarterly*, October 1988, 338–42.

———. "What's Holding Up World Evangelization? The Church Itself." *Evangelical Missions Quarterly*, April 1988, 116–21.

Reed, Lyman E. *Preparing Missionaries for Intercultural Communication: A Bicultural Approach*. Pasadena: William Carey, 1985.

Ridley, Charles R. *How to Select Church Planters*. Pasadena: Fuller Evangelistic Association, 1988.

Robbins, Richard H. *Cultural Anthropology: A Problem-Based Approach*. 2nd ed. Itasca, IL: Peacock, 1997.

Rowen, Samuel F. "Missiology and the Coherence of Theological Education." In *With an Eye on the Future: Development and Mission in the 21st Century*, edited by Duane Elmer and Lois McKinney, 93–100. Monrovia, CA: MARC, 1996.

———. "Should We Drop the Term 'Missionary'?" *Evangelical Missions Quarterly* 7 (1971) 92–98.

Sawatsky, Ben. "What It Takes to Be a Church Planter." *Evangelical Missions Quarterly* 27 (1991) 338–42.

Schnabel, Eckhard J. *Early Christian Mission: Paul and the Early Church.* Vol. 2. Downers Grove: InterVarsity, 2004.

Sills, David M. *Reaching and Teaching: A Call to Great Commission Obedience.* Chicago: Moody, 2010.

Smalley, William. "Cultural Implications of an Indigenous Church." In Winter and Hawthorne, *Perspectives on the World Christian Movement*, 474–79.

———. "Missionary Language Learning in a World Hierarchy of Languages." *Missiology* 22 (1994) 481–88.

Smallman, William H. *Able to Teach Others Also: Nationalizing Global Ministry Training.* Pasadena: Mandate, 2001.

Spitters, Denny, and Matthew Ellison. *When Everything Is Missions.* [Mumbai?]: Bottomline Media, 2017.

Steffen, Tom A. "Missiological Education for the 21st Century." *Evangelical Missions Quarterly* 29 (1993) 178–83.

———. "Missiology's Journey for Acceptance in the Educational World." *Missiology* 31 (2003) 131–53.

———. *Passing the Baton: Church Planting That Empowers.* La Habra, CA: Center for Organizational & Ministry Development, 1997.

———. "Selecting a Church Planting Model That Works. *Missiology* 22 (1994) 361–76.

Stetzer, Ed. *Planting New Churches in a Postmodern Age.* Nashville: Broadman & Holman, 2003.

Stott, John R. W. "The Bible in World Evangelization." In Winter and Hawthorne, *Perspectives on the World Christian Movement*, 31–36.

Taylor, William David, ed. *Global Missiology for the 21st Century: The Iguassu Dialogue.* Grand Rapids: Baker Academic, 2000.

———. "Go Adequately Equipped: You Will Need Training to Serve Well." *Into All the World* (magazine), 2003/4, 37–41.

———. "How Shall We Equip the Cross-Cultural Force?" *Evangelical Missions Quarterly* 29 (1993) 242–48.

———, ed. *Internationalizing Missionary Training: A Global Perspective.* Grand Rapids: Baker, 1991.

———. "Revisiting a Provocative Theme: The Attrition of Longer-Term Missionaries." *Missiology* 30 (2002) 67–80.

———, ed. *Too Valuable to Lose: Exploring the Causes and Cures of Missionary Attrition.* Pasadena: William Carey, 1997.

Thompson, J. Allen. "Church Planter Competencies as Perceived by Church Planters and Assessment Center Leaders: A Protestant North American Study." PhD diss., Trinity Evangelical Divinity School, 1995.

———. "Training Church Planters: A Competency-Based Learning Model." In *With an Eye on the Future: Development and Mission in the 21st Century,* edited by Duane Elmer and Lois McKinney, 141–52. Monrovia, CA: MARC, 1996.

Tiessen, Terrance L. *Who Can Be Saved? Reassessing Salvation in Christ and World Religions.* Downers Grove: InterVarsity, 2004.

Tippett, Alan. "Anthropology: Luxury or Necessity for Missions?" *Evangelical Missions Quarterly* 5 (1968) 7–19.

Van Rheenen, Gailyn. "A Change of Life." MR #31. Missiology.com (blog). May 29, 2003. http://www.missiology.org/blog/GVR-MR-31-A-Change-of-Life.

———. "The Missional Helix: Example of Church Planting." MR #26. Missiology.com (blog). January 20, 2011. http://www.missiology.org/blog/GVR-MR-26-The-Missional-Helix-Example-of-Church-Planting.

———. *Missions: Biblical Foundations & Contemporary Strategies.* Grand Rapids: Zondervan, 1996.

———. "Qualities of Effective Missionaries." MR #10. Missiology.com (blog). October 11, 2000. http://www.missiology.org/blog/GVR-MR-10-Qualities-of-Effective-Missionaries.

Wagner, Peter C. *Frontiers in Mission Strategy.* Chicago: Moody, 1971.

Walls, Andrew. *The Cross-Cultural Process in Christian History.* Maryknoll: Orbis, 2002.

———. *The Missionary Movement in Christian History: Studies in the Transmission of Faith.* Maryknoll: Orbis, 1996.

Ward, Ted. "Educational Preparation of Missionaries—A Look Ahead." *Evangelical Missions Quarterly* 23 (1987) 398–404.

Weber, Hans-Ruedi. "Confronting the World with the Gospel." In *Scripture and Strategy: The Use of the Bible in Postmodern Church and Mission,* edited by David J. Hesselgrave, 87–103. EMS series 1. Pasadena: William Carey, 1994.

Windsor, Raymond, ed. *World Directory of Missionary Training Programmes.* Pasadena: William Carey, 1995.

Winter, Ralph D. "Eleven Frontiers of Perspective (7–11): Part 11." *International Journal of Frontier Missions* 20 (2003) 135–41.

———. "The New Macedonia: A Revolutionary New Era in Missions Begins." In Winter and Hawthorne, *Perspectives on the World Christian Movement,* 339–53.

———. "Re-amateurization of Mission." *Mission Frontiers* 26 (2004) 4–5.

Winter, Ralph D., and Steve C. Hawthorne, eds. *Perspectives on the World Christian Movement: A Reader.* 3rd ed. Pasadena: William Carey, 1999.

Wood, Skevington A. *Ephesians.* Expositor's Bible Commentary 11. Grand Rapids: Zondervan, 1978.